T0167399

If These WALLS Could TALK:
SAN FRANCISCO 49ERS

If These WALLS *Could* TALK:

SAN FRANCISCO 49ERS

Stories from the San Francisco 49ers Sideline, Locker Room, and Press Box

Matt Barrows

TRIUMPH
B O O K S

Library of Congress Cataloging-in-Publication Data

Names: Barrows, Matt, author.
Title: If these walls could talk. San Francisco 49ers : stories from the San Francisco 49ers sideline, locker room, and press box / Matt Barrows.

Other titles: San Francisco 49ers
Description: Chicago : Triumph Books, 2020. | Summary: "This book is about the San Francisco 49ers football club"—Provided by publisher.
Identifiers: LCCN 2020018423 (print) | LCCN 2020018424 (ebook) | ISBN 9781629378022 (paperback) | ISBN 9781641255264 (epub)
Subjects: LCSH: San Francisco 49ers (Football team)—History.
Classification: LCC GV956.S3 B38 2020 (print) | LCC GV956.S3 (ebook) | DDC 796.332/640979461—dc23
LC record available at https://lccn.loc.gov/2020018423
LC ebook record available at https://lccn.loc.gov/2020018424

This book is available in quantity at special discounts for your group or organization. For further information, contact:

Triumph Books LLC
814 North Franklin Street
Chicago, Illinois 60610
(312) 337-0747
www.triumphbooks.com

Printed in U.S.A.
ISBN: 978-1-62937-802-2
Design by Amy Carter
Page production by Sadie Teper

Hi, Mom!

"Attack each day with an enthusiasm unknown to mankind."

—Jim Harbaugh

CONTENTS

FOREWORD

During my NFL career, I've cried twice after a football game. The first time was on February 3, 2013. I remember sitting with our offensive line coach, Mike Solari, in the locker room after the Super Bowl and burying my head into his arms, bawling, and saying, "I'm sorry we couldn't get this done. I'm sorry."

The second time was on February 2, 2020. With about 30 seconds left in the game, I was choking back tears and knew that I had to get off the field as soon as the game was over. I was walking back to the locker room and fighting back tears and then I opened the locker room door and saw my former teammate, Frank Gore. I gave him a big hug and just lost it. Thinking back now, that's why I love this sport. It brings out so much emotion—good and bad—and there's so much that goes into what we do for a living behind the scenes.

This book, *If These Walls Could Talk: San Francisco 49ers*, is about the emotional roller coasters the 49ers have been on in recent years. It's not about the Bill Walsh-era 49ers or the five Super Bowl titles the team has won. It's about the last 20 years of the team, about guys like Gore, Alex Smith, and Justin Smith, and all the great stories we had and the most memorable games we played in together. It's mostly about two teams that were good enough to win a Super Bowl and the climbs we took to get there.

When I think back on those two Super Bowl teams I was a part of— the 2012 team coached by Jim Harbaugh and the 2019 squad coached by Kyle Shanahan—the thing that stands out the most are the differences. The success we had with Harbaugh was so sudden. There was no build-up. There was no long process. The pieces already were in place. It just needed the right coaching staff. We had a lot of talented players on the roster like Gore, Alex Smith, Vernon Davis, and Delanie Walker. The defense was anchored by two of the greatest players of my generation, Justin Smith and Patrick Willis. But we just didn't know that we were as good as we were at that point because we hadn't had a lot of team success. I guess we didn't realize what we could be. And when Harbaugh got here, we started winning almost immediately. It suddenly was clear to us that we were a really good team. We gained a little bit of confidence early on, and it just snowballed from there. The difference was Harbaugh and the coaching staff. It seemed like they were the catalyst.

The most recent team didn't start out that way. This team was built from the ground up. General manager John Lynch and Coach Shanahan came in at the same time and made sure everything was carefully placed together with one vision in mind. It's been built piece by piece by piece. And that's what's so exciting about the current team: I think it's going to be consistent.

It wasn't built with the thought that we had to win right away. No one said, "Hey, all we need to do is add a playmaker" or "We need to go after this guy in free agency." That's what was so exciting to hear from Shanahan and Lynch when they first got here in 2017. You weren't going to win them over with only great numbers, combine scores, or 40-yard dash times. They wanted guys who knew how to play team football. They wanted guys who—even if they weren't in the exact role they wanted—still wanted to be on the field because they liked to compete. And they worked very hard to bring that kind of player in here. They don't always have the flashiest numbers or the most unbelievable athleticism, but you know that you can count on them to be consistent, you know the effort that they're going to bring, and you know they're going to be coachable.

That's why Lynch is so good at what he does. In his job you really have to understand character. It's not like other sports where there is more of an individual aspect. There are 53 guys who all have to pull in the same direction to get us where we want to go. There's so much nuance in our sport, so much technique, so much work, and so much time off. And Lynch lived that. He played in the NFL for 15 seasons. He's not only been around a lot of really high-level players, but he also was a Super

Bowl champion. He clearly understands the dynamic of a championship culture and what it takes to be successful in the NFL.

Then you couple the roster Lynch built with a coaching staff who knows the game like this one does. I've been saying this constantly over the past few years: Shanahan's a genius when it comes to the Xs and Os, how everything gets pieced together on offense, and his overall hold on the entire team. Defensive coordinator Robert Saleh really came into his own this past season, and it showed by how our defense performed week in and week out. Longtime veterans like me and cornerback Richard Sherman may have been frustrated at times in recent years. I'm sure Sherman wasn't used to it because he had never really experienced any kind of losing season like the one we had in 2018. But we also could sense that this success was coming. We had a lot of confidence because even during those difficult seasons everyone was working hard every day, and no one was split. And that kind of stuff goes a long way.

The other aspect that I love about this team is the communication. It's been excellent and it's been direct. And it all starts with the general manager and head coach. Everybody's pulling in the same direction. They might not always agree, and there will be fights here and there, but everyone has the same vision. Hopefully, this current run lasts a long time. I'm optimistic it will.

—*Joe Staley*
49ers offensive tackle (2007–2019)

CHAPTER 1
BLEAK SEASONS

A reporter once made a joke about the San Francisco 49ers: the magnificent franchise Eddie DeBartolo Jr., Bill Walsh, and Joe Montana had built over a quarter of a century was torn down by a guy named Owen Pochman. And it only took him a few weeks.

If you were in the visitors' locker room at Sun Devil Stadium on October 26, 2003, you might have believed that to be true. The 49ers had just lost 16–13 in overtime to a one-win Arizona Cardinals team, and Pochman, the team's young kicker, was the biggest reason for the loss. The eyes of 52 angry men and a dozen coaches were glaring at him. Anger wafted through the locker room like steam from the shower stalls. Pochman later would describe it as a "tidal wave of hate."

Pochman wasn't merely an unreliable kicker that day. He had become symbolic of what the once-proud 49ers, the franchise that had won five Super Bowl titles in the 1980s and 1990s and that had spent money lavishly every step of the way, had become. By 2003 they were frugal. They were penny-pinchers. They were trying to win on a budget. It wasn't working. And to some in the organization, Pochman, then 26 years old, personified where the franchise was heading. After the first two games of the 2003 season, the 49ers cut their struggling incumbent kicker, Jeff Chandler. They could have replaced him with five-year veteran Brett Conway or any number of more established options. Instead they chose Pochman, a little-known—and low-cost—alternative, who before joining the 49ers only had attempted two long field goals in an NFL game and had missed both.

At first the signing seemed inspired. Pochman made all four field-goal tries in an early-season loss to the Cleveland Browns. After that he began to wobble. He missed an extra point in a one-point loss at the Seattle Seahawks and then he had two attempts blocked—and another sail wide left—in a win against the Tampa Bay Buccaneers, the game that preceded the loss to the Cardinals. Even before the contest in Arizona, Pochman hadn't exactly endeared himself to teammates. He was dating a former *Playboy* Playmate of the Year, had done some modeling of his own, and walked around the 49ers facility with the bearing of a young prince. The veterans didn't like that their new kicker, who hadn't even gone through the rigors of training camp with them, was soaking himself in the hot and cold tubs just as much as the 10-year players who were bruised and beat up from slugging it out every Sunday in the trenches.

All of that came to a boil on a hot afternoon in Tempe, Arizona. Pochman missed his only two field-goal attempts in the game, a 45-yarder early in the second quarter and then a 35-yard try with 2:25 left in regulation that would have given the 49ers a 16–13 lead and a probable victory. Then came his closing act. The kickoff that began the overtime period skidded out of bounds, a penalty that automatically gave the Cardinals the ball at their 40-yard line. Nine plays later, they knocked in a 39-yard field goal for the win. "I've not seen a kicker influence a game as negatively as I saw today, not in my career," said 49ers general manager Terry Donahue, who had signed Pochman a month earlier, in an eerily silent locker room afterward.

Minutes earlier it hadn't been so quiet. Jim Mora, the team's high-strung defensive coordinator, had watched his unit hold Arizona quarterback Jeff Blake to 97 passing yards and the Cardinals to a single touchdown only to have the effort ruined by the kicker. Mora was livid. He exploded on Pochman—and the team's tight-fisted ways—as the 49ers filed into the college locker room, repeatedly referring to Pochman as a high-school kicker. Mora screamed that he wouldn't be able to put his kids through college because the 49ers had signed a budget kicker. The tirade lasted for five minutes, died down so head coach Dennis Erickson could address the team, and then caught fire again. Pochman was getting out of his uniform just a few feet away the entire time.

No one would even look at the kicker. In a book he authored four years later, Pochman noted the ridicule continued on the team bus. Someone had squirted barbecue sauce all over his seat, something

Pochman didn't realize until he got up to start boarding the team plane. He figured he wouldn't last until the next game. He was right. He was cut the next day and replaced with Todd Peterson, a nine-year veteran who stabilized the kicking spot by going 12-of-15 the rest of the season.

The episode, however, only was part of the 49ers' descent.

There was more cost-cutting in the offseason as the team struggled to disentangle itself from the salary cap issues that had been choking it for years. After the 49ers had gone 4–12 in 1999, the team's old guard—Walsh and his excellent personnel executive, John McVay—felt they had made the team respectable again with a nucleus that included quarterback Jeff Garcia, wide receiver Terrell Owens, and running back Garrison Hearst. The 49ers made the playoffs in 2001 and 2002. Owens became a star.

The team's bookkeeping measures in the 2004 offseason, however, claimed all three offensive pillars as well as Derrick Deese and Ron Stone, two of the best players on the offensive line. Donahue, who had become the general manager in 2001, thought he had found their replacements: Tim Rattay at quarterback, Brandon Lloyd at receiver, Kevan Barlow at running back, and Kwame Harris and Justin Smiley along the offensive line.

That group turned out to be poor reproductions of the originals. The 2004 season started off badly. Then it got worse. Then it became comical. The 49ers won just two games that year—both in overtime against the same opponent, the lowly Cardinals. A 49ers team that not only had been the class of the NFL, but also the paragon of all professional sports franchises for the previous two decades, had morphed into a laughingstock. Early in the season, the 49ers were trailing the New York Jets by one point in the Meadowlands. They had driven the ball all the way to New York's 35-yard line late in the fourth quarter, prompting the raspy-voiced Donahue to belt out in the otherwise quiet press box: "Let's go out and win a ballgame!"

No one on the field below shared his enthusiasm. Instead of attempting to go for it on fourth down or trying a go-ahead field goal, the 49ers opted to punt—from the Jets' 35. It turned into a touchback—the 49ers gained only 15 yards on the exchange—in a game the Jets eventually won 22–14.

Later that year, one of the few veterans who hadn't been purged in the offseason, fullback Fred Beasley, complained that his younger teammates weren't taking the games seriously enough. "There are guys who are worried about how long their braids are or how much bling-bling they have," he said of the dismaying conversations he overheard on the plane rides back from road defeats.

Only one player fit that description: Lloyd, whom the 49ers hoped would fill Owens' void. Lloyd only was in his second season at the time but had the arrogance and swagger of a vastly more accomplished player. He wasn't just a football player; he was an aspiring rap star. He wore a sparkling silver chain with a scripted "B" at the end. The "B" was topped by a crown. "Why a crown?" Lloyd was asked.

"I'm the prince," he said with a self-assured grin.

One of the worst losses that year came at the Buccaneers on November 21. The 49ers had a walk-through practice the day before the game after which the players were on their own. One of them, cornerback Jimmy Williams, arrived at the city's famous strip club, Mons Venus, made a few arrangements, and then brought a cab-load of dancers back to the team hotel for a party in his double room. Williams didn't play the next day because of a lingering toe injury. You might say his teammates never truly took the field either. The 49ers fell 35–3. It was the second most lopsided loss in a season that was full of embarrassing blowout defeats. The loss dropped the 49ers to 1–9, prompting a question in the postgame press conference to Erickson as to whether he'd ever coached a 1–9 team before. "If I had, I wouldn't be standing up here," the coach deadpanned. "I'd be bartending some place."

The No. 1 pick in the 2005 NFL Draft, Alex Smith struggled as a young player before coming into his own. (Terrell Lloyd / San Francisco 49ers)

The 49ers finished the season 2–14, a record they hadn't had since 1979, the previous low point in the franchise's history and the year DeBartolo hired Walsh, brought in McVay, and drafted Montana. It was as if the organization had come full circle. The 49ers were at the bottom again. Before the season began, Erickson was told he wouldn't be held responsible for all the talent that had been lopped off during the offseason. But when the 2004 season ended, he was fired, and Donahue followed him out the door. "Nobody expected to be 2–14—no one; 2–14 is just unacceptable," the team's owner, John York said, in a press conference.

At that point the 49ers looked nothing like the sterling organization they had been. Not only had they plummeted to the basement of the league standings, but all of the great minds, leaders, and visionaries had faded from the franchise as well. DeBartolo, the beloved former owner of the team, had been forced to relinquish control to his sister, Denise, and brother-in-law, York, in 2000. McVay had been asked to come back to bring stability through the ownership transition but ultimately retired—this time for good—in 2004. Walsh had served as general manager and then as team consultant for a while but was no longer in that role in 2004. Donahue had been brought in by Walsh and had been his hand-picked successor to run the 49ers front office. Donahue in turn had hired Erickson. When that duo was fired on January 5, 2005, the final ties to the 49ers' glorious past had been severed. The Yorks were on their own. They had to start over.

The initial moves, though, were an echo of the past. The 49ers first hired a head coach, Mike Nolan, who in turn found someone to run his personnel department, the like-minded Scot McCloughan. Together, they settled on a fair-haired quarterback, Alex Smith, with the No. 1 pick in the draft.

Nolan and McCloughan knew how talentless the team had become under Donahue and realized they would struggle early on. They certainly didn't want Smith, only 20 years old at the time of the 2005 draft, compared to a Hall of Fame quarterback like Montana. They needed to manage expectations and bring Smith along slowly. The team's marketing department, however, couldn't resist the delicious parallel. Fans certainly had noticed how far their team had fallen and were voicing their dissatisfaction. The final home game of the awful 2004 season was Fan Appreciation Day at Candlestick Park, which at that point was known as Monster Park, the result of a short-lived naming-rights deal with a nearby technology company. An estimated 30,000 fans—fewer than half the venue's capacity—arrived for the game, and by the end of the 41–7 blowout loss to the Buffalo Bills, there were perhaps only 5,000 remaining. The message: "The 49ers thank the greatest fans in the NFL," ran on the electronic scoreboard at the end of the game, but those who stuck around were only there to boo the team off the field.

After the 49ers hired Nolan and McCloughan and acquired Smith, the 49ers began an ad campaign that focused on the word "faithful," the nickname for the team's fans. In a commercial that ran during the spring and summer when the 49ers were trying to sell season tickets, the character actor Charles Napier—known for playing traditional, tough guy roles like cops or soldiers—played the part of a square-jawed Candlestick Park ticket taker who has been around the team for decades. In the ad the gruff old man refused to let a fan enter the stadium until he answered the question, "Do you believe?"

"Do you believe one draft pick can change everything?" The ticket taker asked. "Do you believe in miracles, that a team can go from 2–14 to the Super Bowl in two years?"

Smith never made an appearance in the spot, but as the ticket taker spoke, images of Montana, Walsh, and the 49ers' first Super Bowl team flashed across the screen. The subtext, of course, was that it doesn't take long for a new head coach and a special quarterback to turn a two-win team into a Super Bowl champion. And that a true fan—a real member of the "Faithful" —would get on board at the ground floor. After all, Walsh and Montana pulled off their miracle in their third season. The fans who bought tickets with the hope that York, Nolan, and the teams they ran could deliver a similar feat would end up waiting a lot longer than that.

CHAPTER 2
TOUGH GUYS

Mike Nolan and Scot McCloughan didn't have much success when they ran the San Francisco 49ers because they never had any continuity on offense. Nolan had a different offensive coordinator in each of his four seasons as head coach and, through his dealings with Alex Smith, he illustrated that he didn't know how to manage a quarterback. There was one area, however, in which the duo excelled. They knew how to find tough guys, something that would be evident when Jim Harbaugh took over years later and found a core of battle-hardened, Pro Bowl-caliber players, who immediately would lead the team to the playoffs. Most had been acquired by Nolan and McCloughan.

Nolan was the son of Dick Nolan, who had been the Dallas Cowboys defensive coordinator in the 1960s and the 49ers head coach in the early 1970s. Of Dick Nolan's six kids, Mike loved football the most and, starting at a young age, he was a mainstay in NFL locker rooms, equipment rooms, and training rooms. When he was seven years old, he watched in awe as Dan Reeves, then a halfback with the Cowboys, was treated for a hip pointer. The Cowboys medical staff whipped Reeves' pants down and then stuck a long needle into his side. To a second grader, it seemed like a harpoon. Mike looked on with wide eyes as the needle disappeared into the player's hip, and the memory would stick with him his entire life. It didn't scare him from the sport nor did an incident in high school when a teammate's finger poked through Nolan's facemask and plunged into his right eye. Teammates gathered around him as a puddle of blood began pooling in the socket. He stayed in the hospital for nearly a week with a detached retina, and today the injured eye is dark brown in color while the other is hazel. Nolan never was able to see as well out of the eye again. But he kept playing, eventually becoming a starting safety at the University of Oregon. He was small but feisty and unafraid to fight. And when he became the 49ers head coach, he knew what to look for when shopping for gritty, overachieving players.

Frank Gore shows his toughness by rushing for 127 yards in a 2011 game against the Philadelphia Eagles when most figured he was too injured to play. (Terrell Lloyd / San Francisco 49ers)

So did McCloughan. While Nolan was the son of an NFL coach, McCloughan was raised by an NFL scout, Kent McCloughan, who started working for the Oakland Raiders in 1972. Scot McCloughan got into the business by working under longtime Green Bay Packers general manager Ron Wolf, who sought big-bodied, tough-minded players and who taught McCloughan how to find the right ones. McCloughan had a might-is-right philosophy that meshed very well with Nolan's.

They started working together in 2005 and immediately found someone so tough and resilient that most think he's destined for the Pro Football Hall of Fame. Running back Frank Gore was a mess before the draft that year. Nolan held a barbecue at his house the day before the event, and McCloughan remembers fielding phone call after phone call from a nervous Gore, who was in Miami at the time. He was worried about when he would be drafted. Different teams were telling him different things. Gore didn't know what to think and was going crazy. "He thought he was going in the first or the second," McCloughan said. "The Cowboys told him they were taking him in the second. Some other team told him they were taking him in the first. I told him, 'Congratulations if they take you that high.' But we couldn't do it."

McCloughan might have been Gore's biggest fan at that point. He had been the Southeast region scout for the Seattle Seahawks four years earlier. When he dropped in on Miami to look at the Hurricanes' sensational running backs, Clinton Portis and Willis McGahee, it was Gore—18 years old at the time—who swept him off his feet. "He was just so natural as a runner," McCloughan said. "I didn't know him as a person then. He just stood out. He had really good suddenness, really good power, he ran low to the ground. He made Portis and McGahee look like backups. And they were great running backs, and he was a true freshman."

By 2005, however, McCloughan knew Gore wasn't going to be drafted early. No team would take that risk. The running back had torn the ACL in both of his knees at Miami and he also had shoulder issues that worried NFL teams. Even if he fully rebounded from those surgeries, team doctors didn't think he'd last long at the most punishing position in football. Many teams scratched him off their draft board altogether or at the very least put a big red cross, one denoting a medical issue, next to his name.

That wasn't the only concern. Gore had scored a six on the Wonderlic intelligence test that most prospects take before the draft. The exam features 50 questions that get progressively more difficult, and test takers usually run out of time—it's 12 minutes long—well before they reach the hardest questions at the end. The first 10, however, are considered easy. For example: is 11:59 PM just before or just after midnight? The initial 10 questions are meant to be answered quickly and are designed to test how well someone can read. Most players score in the low 20s. Any score under 10, however, is a red flag that suggests the prospect has reading or learning issues and that a team might have to consider teaching something like the playbook in a different manner.

Gore also failed to ace his pre-draft workout in front of NFL teams. He arrived at the scouting combine that year weighing 232 pounds and looking as fleshy as a fullback. A few weeks later at Miami's Pro Day, Gore had dropped more than 15 pounds so that he could post a fast time in his 40-yard dash.

Gore had a favorite routine from his high school days in the Miami area. To get in shape, he'd head to the region's Tropical Park, which had the biggest hill—perhaps the only hill—in pancake flat South Florida. He not only ran it forward, backward, and while side-stepping, but he also tied a length of thick rope around his waist and dragged a truck tire—one gradually loaded with weights—up and down the hill. It was a routine he continued even when he was a star with the 49ers and one he did in the summer months when the Florida humidity was at its most oppressive. Whenever it was an unusually hot day in breezy, mild Santa Clara, Gore was in his element. He loved to sweat.

Back in 2005, however, Gore's sudden weight loss didn't allow him to go faster. He had sweated and starved away the pounds so rapidly that he had robbed his own muscles of energy and compromised his power. "He said, 'But I lost all that weight,'" McCloughan said. "I told him, 'You lost all your strength. You can't lose that amount of weight that fast.' He did not eat for like a week and a half straight."

McCloughan clocked Gore at 4.78 seconds when the running back ran his 40-yard dash—a time a lumbering tight end might record—but changed it to 4.72 seconds because Gore was running on grass. McCloughan was doing everything in his power to make the running back seem draftable to the others on the 49ers staff. Two weeks before the draft, he sat down with Nolan and offensive coordinator Mike McCarthy and told them he had settled on who he wanted to take in the third round: Frank Gore. McCarthy was skeptical. "The kid who can't stay healthy?" McCloughan remembers McCarthy saying. "If you say so."

Back at Nolan's barbecue the day before the draft, McCloughan explained to Gore over the phone that he couldn't take him in the first two rounds. "But I can ball!" Gore pleaded.

McCloughan told the running back he knew he was special and assured him that if he was still there in the third round he would become a 49er. That's what the 49ers did despite having a tailback, Kevan Barlow, who had rushed for nearly 2,000 yards and scored 13 touchdowns over the two prior seasons. That McCloughan kept his word earned him lifetime loyalty from Gore. The two still talk on the phone once a week. The running back also acutely remembered everyone who passed on him and quickly memorized the names of the five running backs who were drafted before him: Ronnie Brown, Cedric Benson, Cadillac Williams, J.J. Arrington, and Eric Shelton.

Gore vowed not to let any of them outrush him in their careers. None came close. And 15 years after the draft, Gore still can recite the list in the order the players were drafted. The last runner from the group to remain in the NFL, Brown, made his final carry on December 20, 2014, in a game, fittingly, against the 49ers. Brown had seven carries for 33 yards that day; Gore finished with 26 carries for 158 yards, including a 52-yard touchdown. "I'm the last one now," Gore noted in 2017.

The injury issues that prompted teams to erase his name from their draft boards in 2005 never were problematic. Gore missed five games in 2010 with a fractured hip he suffered when he fell awkwardly in a game against the Arizona Cardinals. Otherwise, the saying around 49ers headquarters was that you could count on three things in life: death, taxes, and Frank Gore rushing for 1,200 yards. In 2016 Gore, then 33 and a member of the Indianapolis Colts, became the oldest player since John Riggins in 1984 to run for 1,000 yards in a season.

Norv Turner was the 49ers' offensive coordinator in 2006, the season Gore rushed for a career-high 1,695 yards, the best in the NFC that year. Turner had coached Emmitt Smith, the NFL's all-time rushing leader who played 15 seasons. Turner noted a similarity: both runners were adept at tucking in behind their blockers and running so low to the ground that they avoided the massive body blows that shortened others' careers. "He's a very, very smart player, he's got the low center of gravity, and he's so powerful in his lower body," Turner said. "He had all the ingredients that it takes to be a top running back."

Turner wasn't the only coach who came away thinking Gore was "very, very smart." The learning issues some fretted about before the draft never materialized. He quickly picked up the playbook and never was out of position. In fact, it was usually Gore, who with his view from his tailback spot, was first to realize when a teammate had lined up incorrectly and either called a timeout or quickly ushered that player into the right place in the formation. "During the season I'd usually get into my office around 6:30," Gore's running backs coach, Tom Rathman, said. "And he was in my office at 7:00, even though our first meeting didn't start until 8:30. For him it was, 'What's different? What are the protections this week? What do they do with their blitzes?' He was so enamored with learning what [the opponent] was doing so that he could get ahead, so he could stay ahead of the game. I never had another player do that."

Mostly, Gore excelled because he loved football like nothing else in the world. He even cherished the most mundane details of his job. Few tailbacks, for example, enjoy their role as pass protectors, and most are reluctant blockers. Gore had a passion for it, which he loved to show off. The offensive linemen sometimes were gathered in their meeting room when Gore would pop in with a laptop, dying to show them a block he had made in a game. After all, who appreciates a good block more than an offensive lineman? "He would get so excited about the blocks that he made. He'd come into the o-line room and be like, 'Fellas, check this out!'" Adam Snyder, a guard who was part of the same draft class as Gore, said. "The thing about him that was most impressive to me was not his running because everyone knows he's a great runner. But his pass protection was unbelievable. He would just lay dudes out."

That happened—twice in quick succession—during a joint practice between the 49ers and Raiders in 2009 at Oakland's training camp home in Napa Valley. The one-on-one pass-blocking drills that coaches run in practice favor the linebackers over the running backs. After all, they're bigger. And they get a running start while the running back has to try to hold his ground and keep the blitzing linebacker away from his quarterback. When Raiders linebacker Ricky Brown approached Gore, however, it was as if he was hit by a sledgehammer. Gore put the linebacker on his back and then did the same to the next challenger. He was so fired up in the drill that he had to be pulled away from the angry Raiders defensive players. Rathman waded into the scrum, yelling for another running back to come in and take Gore's place. It was for the Raiders' protection. "This was an ass whuppin'," Rathman recalled of the drill. "It happened twice, and both times I had to jump in and take him off the guy because he was going to keep finishing him."

The head coach at the time, Mike Singletary, enjoyed the stir Gore caused. "I love the emotion, I love the enthusiasm," Singletary said. "That's the game. That's passion. If I told him to stop doing that, he couldn't. That's just who Frank is. He's a competitor. Everything he does, he does it with his heart. That really is the thing that sets him apart."

Cowboy's Last Ride

Justin Smith's tenure with the San Francisco 49ers began in 2008 with a helicopter ride, which in hindsight seems like an odd activity for a decidedly no-frills defensive end from rural Missouri nicknamed

Cowboy. At the time, though, Smith was the most coveted player in free agency. The 49ers wanted to give him an experience no other suitor could offer. Their goal was to make sure he didn't get back on a plane and visit the Minnesota Vikings, the Jacksonville Jaguars, or any other team that was courting him that offseason.

So Smith and Nolan hopped on a helicopter that took them over the city of San Francisco, Alcatraz Island, the Golden Gate Bridge, and then back down the majestic California coastline toward the South Bay. It was fun, Smith said later, but that wasn't what sold him on the 49ers. Instead, it was a dinner he had with the team's defensive coordinator at the time, Greg Manusky. The two drank cheap beer until early in the morning, trading hunting and drinking stories and going over how Manusky planned to utilize the defensive end in his system. It was near dawn by the time they were through. A slightly tipsy Manusky called Scot McCloughan and bragged about the free agent he had just bagged. "We got him!" Manusky happily exclaimed.

Smith liked the plan the 49ers had for him. When he began his career with the Cincinnati Bengals in 2001, he was a 265-pound defensive end who played on the outside of the line on all three downs. The 49ers were eying him as a defensive end on running downs and as someone who could play inside—and use his strength and quickness against guards—on passing downs. Smith, who would eventually bulk up to 295 pounds, thought that was a good idea.

He also liked the collaboration he had with defensive line coach Jim Tomsula, who gave him and his defensive linemates a degree of autonomy when on the field he hadn't had to that point in his career. Instead of being locked into a particular formation that hinged on the offense's personnel, Tomsula—and later defensive coordinator Vic Fangio—gave Smith some wiggle room based on what he was seeing and hearing on the field. After all, he was only inches away from his opponents. The coaches were all the way on the sideline, and Fangio was up in the coaches' booth.

"You can really hear what's going on in the inside," Smith said. "The center is making the calls. You see where they're sliding and you see how you can beat a protection. The coaches can't hear that. And you know, they were kind of leery at first. They were, 'How the hell do you know?' Well, because they're telling us. We can hear it. Then [the coaches] finally started listening to us. Jimmy T was awesome as far as taking some input and listening to us…Vic, Jimmy T, all those guys, they were just awesome in giving us some input. And that was the first time in my career I'd ever had that."

Smith was a newcomer in 2008, but he quickly became the ringleader on the field and in the locker room. He was Paul Bunyan in a football helmet, a guy with forearms like fence posts and a work ethic like no other. He was a good storyteller and served as an excellent mentor to the younger players on the team. There was, of course, no coddling. Cowboy might have been the most intimidating guy on the team. No one dared cross him. You merely followed his lead. He also was the center of the team's nightlife, which is what you'd expect from a charismatic country boy with an Anheuser-Busch tattoo on his left arm.

Teammates tell a story about Smith's first offseason with the team. At the time left tackle Joe Staley, who had been a first-round pick the year earlier, had another offensive lineman, Jeb Terry, staying at his house in Campbell, California. One weekend Staley flew back to his boyhood home in Michigan to attend his sister's graduation. Terry asked if he could have a couple of the other offensive lineman—Adam Snyder and David Baas—over for a couple of beers in his absence. "No problem," Staley said. "Just don't break anything."

The small get-together began in the afternoon and turned into a night-time affair. It also expanded in size, and soon Smith and his rowdy defensive line crew arrived. At some point, Smith noticed there was a small firepit next to the pool in Staley's stylishly designed backyard.

"Hey, it's kind of chilly tonight," he said, according to teammates who were on hand. "Let's get a fire going. Let's crank this thing up!"

So they started throwing the firewood that was neatly stacked nearby into the pit and pretty soon had a nice, warm blaze going. After a while the party was still rolling, but the fire had died down. Smith called out for someone to throw a few more logs into the pit. They said they couldn't because there was no more firewood. "The hell there isn't," Smith said.

He stepped away and came back with a chaise lounge from Staley's teak pool furniture set and tossed it into the pit. It immediately burst into flames. "And everybody's like, 'You can't do it! You can't do it!'" Alex Smith, one of the partygoers and a close friend of Staley's, said. "And then he chucked it in. And this thing lights up. It lights up so big and burns so hot and fast. And everyone's having fun with it, roaring and raving, and the flames are leaping up like six feet high. And this [pit] is below ground, so there are some big flames coming out. But then it burned out pretty quick. Like two minutes later, it's out."

For Justin Smith that was merely the beginning of the fireworks. He went and found another piece of furniture and then another, stacking them until the flames were nearly as high as the house. "And the next thing you know, we'd burned his entire patio furniture set," Alex Smith recalled. "There had to be like 15 pieces of furniture out there that we burned—chairs and a table. It was ridiculous. And once we started burning bigger pieces of furniture, there were these huge flames. And we're all taking pictures of this stuff and sending them to Joe: 'Does this look familiar?'"

"Well, yeah, we ran out of firewood," Justin Smith said when asked if the story was true. "And he had some teak furniture. I was new to the team and I was like, 'Just burn this young guy's furniture.'"

How does teak burn? "Pretty damn good if I remember right," Smith said. "I guess it had some lacquer on it or something."

Staley, of course, was 2,000 miles away, but he started getting texts from amused, possibly concerned, and definitely inebriated partygoers. "I remember getting a text early in the night from Damane Duckett," Staley said. "And all it said was, 'Where you at?'"

Staley looked at the message, didn't think anything of it, and got ready for bed. The texts, however, continued to pour in. "Then I go to the bathroom in the middle of the night and remember checking my phone," he said. "It was a text from Alex Smith. And it said, 'Where are you?' And it was a picture of all my furniture in my backyard going up in flames. And the flames were like 15 feet high. I kept getting all these pictures. And I lived in a residential community. It wasn't like I had a big backyard. And the flames were, like, shooting up toward my house."

When Staley got back from Michigan, he walked into his backyard and saw that all of his patio furniture, including an outdoor bar set, had been stacked like cordwood in the fire pit. "It didn't even burn all the way," he said. "It was just the skeleton of the furniture."

Justin Smith laughs about the episode. In his defense, he noted that the 49ers players weren't hanging out together at that time. He was merely trying to make them a closer group. He also says he was trying to toughen up the young guy a little bit. Staley, after all, only was 23. He had bought his first house a year earlier. "I mean, you could imagine a young guy coming home and finding his new furniture burnt like that," Justin Smith said. "That stuff gets to you when you're young like that, for sure. When I was younger, they used to mess with me for damn sure. You used to have to bring food in every Friday. It wasn't like it is now. There wasn't always constant food and chefs like they have now. So you had to constantly bring food in, take the guys out to eat every Friday night—if you were a rookie—at a steakhouse."

Since the bonfire was all Justin Smith's idea, Staley eventually worked up the nerve and confronted the veteran defensive lineman and told him he owed him for the furniture. "And Justin's like, 'All right. Whatever.'

And he wrote him a check for like a thousand bucks," offensive lineman Daniel Kilgore said. "Well, that furniture was like 12 grand. And Joe never had the nerve to say anything about it."

Justin Smith recalled that Staley approached him. "Oh yeah, he was kind of worried about it," Smith said. "But I was just laughing about it. So I gave him a check for whatever he wanted. It toughened him up. He went on a hell of a run. I'll take some pride in that. I paid Joe for those things. Don't let him say I didn't."

Bamm-Bamm

"Who in the fuck is 52?" Chad Johnson, the normally outspoken Cincinnati Bengals receiver, was nearing the end of a rather boring, lifeless—and decidedly quote-less—conference call interview with Bay Area reporters before a game against the San Francisco 49ers in 2007 when he suddenly remembered something that made him perk up. And with Johnson, *up* meant that his energy level lurched from a 2 to near reactor-meltdown conditions in a half second. "Oh, my fucking God! I done seen a lot of linebackers in a seven-year period," he screeched into the phone…You guys can laugh all you want. He is the real deal! He's playing with a cast on his hand, right? All during film I'm calling him Bamm-Bamm like from *The Flintstones* because he's just hitting everything."

By that point in the season, everyone in the Bay Area knew exactly who No. 52 was. But Patrick Willis, the 49ers' rookie linebacker, was just starting to catch fire nationally. Three weeks earlier, Willis had turned in one of the best plays of the 2007 NFL season. It would end up as perhaps the finest tackle in a career that would include nearly 1,000 of them and it was a perfect example of what made him unique.

With the score tied at 31 in overtime in Arizona, it looked like the Cardinals would score an all-too-easy touchdown when Kurt Warner threw from his own 14-yard line and hit receiver Sean Morey on a short pass outside the numbers. There were no 49ers defenders near him and no one between him and the end zone. It was a busted coverage at a critical moment. It seemed as if the 5'11", 193-pound slot receiver was gone. Willis, however, took off like a big cat after its prey and steadily gained ground until he pounced on the rabbit-quick Morey at the 49ers' 24-yard line, some 62 yards from where the play began. The speed he displayed was awesome and, as it turned out, the tackle was critical. Instead of winning with a touchdown, the Cardinals blew a short field-goal attempt. When Arizona got the ball again in overtime, the 49ers defense struck once more, and a sack and fumble recovery in the end zone gave them a dramatic 37–31 victory. "After the first few yards, I said, 'I can get this guy. I just gotta run, I just gotta put the head back,'" Willis said a few days after the game. "I was going to go for [the tackle] earlier, but then I saw the ball and I said, 'No, the best thing to do is try to get on him a little bit closer to make the sure tackle.'"

The same play had Johnson in near hysterics a few weeks later. "The one we watched on film, he runs down the guy from Arizona from behind," he said, "that's unheard of. But other than that, No. 52, I can't even say anything more. His play speaks for itself... He's the truth. You just tell him 85 said, 'You're the truth.' I stopped watching the DBs to watch him. I don't know anything about playing the position, but I know when someone is doing something right because he is making every damn play."

Against the Arizona Cardinals, Willis didn't quite make every damn play. But he did finish with 18 tackles, an absurd number for any defensive player—let alone a rookie playing with a plaster club protecting a broken right hand. It was the most for a 49ers player since 1994 when the league started keeping track of tackle totals. Later in his rookie season, he had a 20-tackle game in a win against the Tampa Bay Buccaneers.

For long stretches of the 2007 season, a year in which the starting quarterback was injured and the team finished with five wins, Willis was the only thing worth watching on the 49ers. He was a ray of light in a pitch black season. He and Dave Wilcox, who played from 1964 to 1974 and was voted into the Pro Football Hall of Fame in 2000, are arguably the top two linebackers in 49ers history. Yet not everyone was a believer right away. The 49ers coaching staff got an early look at Willis when they coached the South team at the Senior Bowl in January of 2007. Mike Singletary, who at the time was the 49ers linebackers coach, wasn't all that impressed. Head coach Mike Nolan also needed to be convinced. Willis, after all, wasn't very imposing. He was about 230 pounds during the week of Senior Bowl practices, he had suffered a couple of broken bones at Ole Miss, and he didn't always take on the blocks of guards and centers, preferring instead to go around them to get to the ball carrier.

Singletary, of course, had played middle linebacker in the 1980s and was famously physical. Singletary's era was one in which the offense and defense grappled for dominance in the trenches, a time when establishing the running game—and snuffing it out—was paramount. If a linebacker wasn't stout or gritty enough to bang away with pulling guards, he didn't last long. Singletary questioned whether Willis had the mettle to hold up. Scot McCloughan, however, liked what he saw on film. Willis certainly had been tough enough to lead the talented Southeastern Conference in tackles two years straight, one of them while playing with a club on his hand, which would be a recurring theme in his professional career. "I said, 'Of course he's not taking on blockers,'" McCloughan said in response to Singletary's concern. "'He's got a broken hand!'"

And he had speed. Willis was faster than many wide receivers coming out of the draft that year. As he proved in the Cardinals game, he could run down the ball carrier no matter where he was when the play began. "You don't lead the SEC in tackles two years straight without being pretty damn good," McCloughan said. "He was just so much faster and quicker than anyone on the field. He ran down that running back from Arkansas, the really fast one—Darren McFadden—he ran him down on the sideline like it was nothing."

In the end McCloughan's passion for Willis won out. Two years after the 49ers selected Willis, team owner Jed York touted McCloughan to the crowd during a State of the Franchise event, recounting the time when "Scot stands up on the table and fights against the defensive-oriented head coach and says, 'This is going to be our draft pick.'" At the time Willis was the 49ers' best player, McCloughan had been promoted to general manager, and Nolan had been dismissed from the team.

By 2009 Singletary had become the 49ers head coach. Even then he was still tinkering with Willis. He thought a team's inside linebacker, the center of the defense, needed to be vocal. Singletary certainly was. In fact, he was a gifted orator who had held teammates in a near trance when he spoke. Singletary also coached another No. 52, Baltimore Ravens linebacker Ray Lewis, who had a near mystical speaking style. Lewis could transfix anyone in earshot. Ravens teammates naturally rallied around Lewis and would storm a machine gun nest for him. Willis wasn't like that. He didn't like speaking. He wasn't good at it. He was quiet.

But even though Willis didn't like to talk, there was still something stirring inside. His mother left him and his siblings when Willis was 4 years old, and the children were brought up by their father in rural Western Tennessee. Ernest Willis struggled with drugs and alcohol at various points in his life, and on one occasion, he became so abusive with Patrick's younger sister, Ernicka, that her quiet, studious older brother—still a teenager at the time—stepped in to stop the beating.

Patrick told school counselors what was happening, which led to child protective services taking the Willis children out of Ernest's home. Patrick and his three younger siblings initially were to be sent to a home

70 miles away, but Willis' basketball coach at the time, Chris Finley, stepped in and had them stay with him and his wife in their trailer in Bruceton, Tennessee. Today, Willis refers to Chris and Julie Finley as "Mom and Dad." But Willis always saw himself as his siblings' guardian and protector. When the 49ers drafted him with the 11th overall pick in 2007, Willis was a 22 year old with the temperament and the obligations of an older man.

Despite Willis' lofty draft status, Nolan and Singletary didn't award the rookie linebacker a starting job right away. They were still reluctant and wanted Willis to earn the role. During spring practices and even into training camp, Willis worked with the second-team defense. When he finally was given a chance with the starters, on a rare day when the 49ers wore their full padding in practice, it was as if the coaches had let a tiger loose from its cage. You didn't even need to open your eyes to know the effect Willis was having on the field. You could hear it in the hard plastic of the padding every time Willis—*crack*—shot in against an offensive player. Willis didn't so much hit his opponents as sting them. He made his first start in the team's third preseason game in Chicago against the Bears and led the 49ers with seven tackles. "You just knew," McCloughan recalled of Willis' initial start. "The players, the veterans, were like, 'Holy shit! This guy's legit.'"

Willis never left the starting lineup from that point on. Nolan and Singletary finally were convinced. He went on to finish his rookie season with 174 tackles, which at the time was the highest total in a decade. He was the only 49ers defender to play every defensive snap that year and did so in spite of a broken hand suffered in a midseason road game against the Atlanta Falcons. It was a minor inconvenience. Willis still led the team in tackles that day. "The word 'rolling ball of butcher knives' comes to mind," Brad Childress, then the Minnesota Vikings head coach, said before a game in December 2007. "He is everywhere, sideline to sideline."

Willis ran down wide receivers, toppled tight ends, and even outplayed fellow rookie Adrian Peterson when the Vikings came to town that year. Willis finished that game with a team-high eight tackles as well as a fumble recovery. Peterson, who had set the league ablaze that season, carried the ball 14 times and gained only three yards.

When the season ended, Peterson was named the NFL's Rookie of the Year. Willis was awarded Defensive Rookie of the Year. He was the first 49ers defender since Dana Stubblefield in 1993 to win the honor, but it was a secondary prize to Peterson's award. The running back, however, knew who the better player was when they met that December. "That's a game that sticks in my mind," Peterson said two years later. "It's the worst game of my career. I don't take it lightly. I give praise to San Francisco's defense. They have some good guys. They play football like football should be played on the defensive side of the ball. I felt like I was being attacked by bees in that game."

Alex Smith's Rough Start

One of Alex Smith's favorite movies is *The Shawshank Redemption*. It's the story of a man, Andy Dufresne, who uses patience, persistence, intelligence, and time to escape a terrible, unfair situation. That's how Smith must have felt in 2011 after the San Francisco 49ers finally hired a head coach, Jim Harbaugh, who not only had an offensive background, but who also had been an NFL quarterback. Smith initially landed with the 49ers largely because of his measured, Dufresne-like disposition.

Before the 2005 NFL Draft, the team hosted, enjoyed meals with, and researched the hell out of both Smith and Cal quarterback Aaron Rodgers. Those were the only players the 49ers were considering with the No. 1 pick that year despite the team's insistence at the time that they had plenty of options. That wasn't true. If they used the pick, they definitely were drafting a quarterback.

They liked both players. They didn't love either.

Each candidate was highly intelligent. Smith graduated from the University of Utah in a little more than two years with a degree in economics. He scored a 40 on the Wonderlic intelligence test, one of the highest scores that year. Rodgers' 35 score was nearly as impressive. Both quarterbacks had good right arms, though Rodgers had the better of the two. His arm was special. He put on a show in front of coaches and media at Cal's Pro Day on March 17, 2005, completing all but one of the 92 passes he threw. Mike Nolan and then-Miami Dolphins coach Nick Saban were among the NFL head coaches on hand. "He did extremely well," said Nolan, who acknowledged that Rodgers was the most polished passer in the draft. "I don't think he missed but maybe one throw when it started. Other than that, he put them all right there."

A 49ers fan while growing up in the Northern California town of Chico, Rodgers must have thought he had aced the final exam of the draft process with that Pro Day performance and that he would follow in the footsteps of his boyhood idol Joe Montana. Personality, however, was important to a 49ers team that essentially was starting from scratch. And the quarterbacks' personalities were different. "Alex, I wasn't worried about him at all," Scot McCloughan said. "He was A+."

Rodgers? He came off as a little cocky. He called the coaches—Nolan, McCarthy, and quarterbacks coach Jim Hostler—by their first names. At one point in the pre-draft process, Rodgers went so far as to slap Nolan on the butt. It was a friendly, good-natured gesture. The quarterback had gone out to lunch previously with the 49ers coaches, and everyone had hit it off. But it was a little too familiar, too undisciplined. And the 49ers considered it a demerit. They began leaning toward Smith—not because they disliked Rodgers or doubted he'd be successful but because they knew they were going to struggle as a team. "It was about what kind of personality you wanted knowing what we were going to go through," McCloughan said. "We knew we weren't going to be a very good team at that time. How would the quarterback react when we lost a few games in a row? What would he be like in the locker room if we lost 35–7? We wanted an even-keeled guy in that spot."

That was Smith. When the 49ers coaches went to Salt Lake City to watch him throw, they also had him perform some activities you might see on a grade-school playground: skipping rope, playing four square, hopping on one foot and rolling a ball through his legs. The 49ers wanted to see if he'd become frustrated and tested whether he'd lose his temper. Smith played it cool. "It was awkward," he said at the time. "It was very strange, and we did some drills afterward that were pretty peculiar. I think they wanted to take me out of my comfort zone. They wanted to see how I'd react."

The 49ers also liked that Smith had won over an exceedingly hard-to-please coach at Utah. He had been recruited by Ron McBride and was a freshman when McBride's replacement, Urban Meyer, arrived in Salt Lake City. Smith, who'd been recruited to be a pocket quarterback, wasn't anything like the quarterbacks Meyer had had at Bowling Green. Smith said he remembers initially sitting down with Meyer and watching tape of Bowling Green's Josh Harris, a 245 pounder who plowed over defenders on quarterback power runs. "And I'm 18 years old and 180 pounds dripping wet," he said. "And I'm thinking, *I'm not gonna fit into this. How can I do this?* It was all out of the shotgun. I had never played in the shotgun ever. I had no idea what I was doing back there with the zone read and all this stuff. And Urban—I don't know if he tried to run me out—I wouldn't say that. But he was very much also challenging you. He was challenging everybody, especially being new. He wanted to figure out who everybody was. He didn't recruit any of these kids, especially the quarterbacks, so he definitely was in your face, wanting to see what you were made of, how tough you were, whether you were going to stick. And he definitely ran a lot of people off of the program."

Not Smith. He not only stuck around, he became Meyer's starter in 2003. A year later he was a Heisman Trophy finalist and led the Utes to a win in the Fiesta Bowl. "I liked Alex a lot," McCloughan said. "He'd been through a lot at Utah when Urban got there, and they tried to run him off. And they couldn't run him off."

The 49ers never revealed which way they were leaning. In fact, Nolan said in the weeks before the draft that there were as many as six players the 49ers were considering with the top pick. The team also flew in University of Miami defensive back Antrel Rolle and Michigan wide receiver Braylon Edwards for a round of interviews and had them meet the media. At one point Nolan made a surprise visit into the media trailer where all the reporters worked and polled the beat writers on whom they thought the 49ers were going to take. Of the five guys who were typing away that afternoon, two said Smith, two picked Rodgers, and one guessed Edwards. Nolan and McCloughan had done a great job. No one inside the media trailer knew their target. No one outside knew either.

The intent behind the uncertainty, however, was to drum up interest for the No. 1 pick and to trigger a trade. The 49ers were an atrocious team at the time. They needed as many draft picks as possible, and their best-case scenario was to cash in their No. 1 selection for a slew of lesser ones. That didn't happen. As illustrated by Rodgers' draft day fall, none of the other teams thought all that highly of the two quarterbacks or anyone else that year. They didn't want to pay any of the players what the top selection that year would command. In the days leading up to the draft, the 49ers' phones remained silent. There was little trade chatter. "No one wanted that No. 1 pick," McCloughan said. "I tried like hell."

So the 49ers made Smith the top selection in the draft on April 23, 2005. He was only 20 years old. He'd have to wait another month to legally buy a beer. When he took his first snap in a spring practice, the ball slipped from his grasp and ended up on the ground. It was symbolic of a player the 49ers instinctively knew would need time—a lot of time—to become an effective starting quarterback in the NFL.

The initial strategy was to have Smith apprentice behind veteran Tim Rattay during his rookie season. It was a wise decision. Every expert, including Meyer, agreed that was the way to handle Smith. Of course, it only took a few games to rip that plan to pieces. Those tactics always fall apart when a team is losing and its fans wonder why the first-round quarterback, to whom the team is paying millions of dollars, is holding a clipboard on the sideline. So during a nationally televised game in Mexico City in Week Four, the 49ers fell behind the Arizona Cardinals 31–14, and Smith was sent in in the fourth quarter.

He made his first start the next week against Peyton Manning and the Indianapolis Colts. The results were predictable. Manning looked like a future Hall of Famer. Smith was like a newborn foal trying to walk for the first time. He threw four interceptions, was sacked five times, and posted an 8.5 passer rating. He didn't throw his first touchdown pass until the final week of the season, and the 49ers, the franchise that boasted Joe Montana and Steve Young, finished last in the league in passing yards for the first time in club history.

It would get worse from there.

Two years later Smith already was operating under his third different offensive coordinator. The 49ers were playing the Seattle Seahawks in Week Four. On the game's third snap, defensive tackle Rocky Bernard fired through the line of scrimmage unblocked. Smith tried to duck out of the lineman's grasp, but Bernard pounced on his back and his momentum—plus his 308-pound weight—drove Smith into the turf, and Smith's right shoulder bore the brunt of the impact. Smith eventually got up, but his throwing arm was painfully dislodged from the socket. It was diagnosed as a Grade 3 shoulder separation, which meant that the ligaments between his clavicle and shoulder had been torn, and there was a clear separation between the two.

The injury also opened a gulf between Nolan and his quarterback. As Smith tried to return to the lineup, Nolan continually downplayed the shoulder situation, insinuating that the issue was little more than soreness. As the leader of the team, Smith merely needed to grit his teeth and play through the discomfort. "Everybody is sore. I'm sore," Nolan said. "Has that affected my performance? Maybe, but I'm not going to talk about it."

Smith, in turn, said the shoulder wasn't sore. It was "killing" him, and he later had surgery to repair the damaged ligaments. He went on to accuse the head coach of undermining him in the locker room and the 49ers of soft-pedaling the severity of his issue. The quarterback sat out the 2008 season. After the 49ers began the year 2–5, Nolan was fired and replaced by Mike Singletary, who would have his own battles with Smith.

Singletary was a talented orator. That's why Nolan had brought him with him from the Baltimore Ravens when the 49ers made Nolan their head coach in 2005. Not only had Singletary played middle linebacker at a Pro Bowl level and for perhaps the greatest defense in NFL history—the 1985 Chicago Bears—he was someone for whom players would lay siege to a castle if asked. His glorious, booming elocution was on full display after his first game as interim head coach in 2008, one in which Vernon Davis was flagged for a personal foul in a game against the Seahawks. On the sideline Singletary confronted the underachieving tight end, who had been taken with the No. 6 overall pick the year after the 49ers had taken Smith. Singletary banished Davis to the locker room with more than 10 minutes remaining. "I'd rather play with 10 people and just get penalized all the way until we have to do something else rather than play with 11 when I know that right now that person is not sold out to be a part of this team," Singletary railed in the postgame press conference when asked about Davis' exit.

It was as if he were on the pulpit giving a fire-and-brimstone sermon. His parishioners ate it up. "It is more about them than it is about the team," Singletary roared, "cannot play with them, cannot win with them, cannot coach with them, can't do it. I want winners. I want people that want to win."

The incident marked a turning point for Davis. He was a fantastic 49ers tight end from that point forth. He went on to score touchdowns in each of the next two contests. The following season he had a career-high 13 touchdowns and was on the receiving end of one of the 49ers' greatest plays of this century in the 2011 playoffs.

Singletary squeezed success out of Davis, prodded him to his full potential. Like Nolan, however, he didn't know the formula for quarterbacks. At one point, Singletary referred to Smith as "meek." He later corrected himself, saying the word he meant to use was "humble." But the slip revealed both how he viewed Smith and how he misunderstood the quarterback. During a 2010 game against the Philadelphia Eagles, Singletary gave Smith the same treatment he had given Davis two years earlier. On national television he ripped into him on the sideline, desperately wanting to build a fire in his seemingly cool quarterback.

That wasn't what Smith was missing. His temper didn't need to be stimulated; his brain did. Smith craved knowledge, an Xs and Os system that could match his intellect. Singletary, who never had been a defensive coordinator at any level of football, couldn't provide that. Neither could his offensive coordinator, Jimmy Raye, who at that point was the fifth offensive coordinator Smith had been under. Singletary had gotten it wrong. Smith wasn't meek. He wasn't a pushover. He certainly wasn't a wimp, as Nolan implied. He was every bit as willful—and as tough—as they were. He just never let it boil to the surface like they did.

His mother, Pam, tells a story about what Smith was like as a toddler. The 3-year-old Alex Smith was nothing like the adult he is today. He was headstrong, stubborn, and, well, a little tyrant. He once wound himself into a screaming fit so wild and so prolonged that his father, Doug, had to take him into the shower and let cold water wash over his son—anything to cool the boy's scalding temper. At some point he transformed into the polite, moderate, and lovely personality that prompted the 49ers to take him with the top pick. But underneath all of that, Smith remains the obstinate, relentless person he was as a child. It's what allowed him to persevere through the losing seasons, the sacks—he went down 172 times between 2005 and 2011—and the injuries that accompanied them. And it's what allowed him to outlast Nolan and then Singletary, who was fired before the end of the 2010 season.

When Harbaugh took over the next season, and especially after his initial year, Smith never seemed more like the level-headed Dufresne. He had survived a quarterback's nightmare scenario. He had crawled to freedom through 500 yards of shit-smelling foulness and had come out clean on the other side. Or so he thought.

CHAPTER 3
CAMP ALEX

When Jim Harbaugh, Greg Roman, and the new San Francisco 49ers coaching staff took over on January 7, 2011, everyone assumed the group would bring in a new quarterback. Incoming regimes, after all, nearly always take over dilapidated squads and they usually want a hand-picked signal caller to be the foundation of their rebuild. Harbaugh and the 49ers had the seventh overall pick in a draft that, at least at the time, was thought to be teeming with talented quarterbacks like Cam Newton, Jake Locker, Blaine Gabbert, and Christian Ponder. There also was a case to be made for Alex Smith burnout in the Bay Area. He was supposed to have been the team's savior—the centerpiece of the last rebuild—when the 49ers picked him No. 1 overall six years earlier. He had thrown 51 touchdowns against 53 interceptions since, never had taken the team to the playoffs, and never had even piloted the team to a winning record.

His college coach, Urban Meyer, preached patience with Smith, noting that he was a cerebral and deliberate player. On the day Smith was drafted, the 49ers arranged for Meyer to speak with reporters on a conference call. Those sessions are usually filled with flowery, empty praise from the former head coach, whose own worth is reflected in the glory of his protege. College coaches talk about their quarterbacks like they're first-born sons. Meyer, however, surprised everyone with his frankness. He said the methodical Smith would be "non-functional" until he learned an entire offense. Meyer said plenty of wonderful things about Smith, too. And he said once a system truly clicked in the quarterback's mind that he would be fantastic. *But non-functional?* The adjective lingered. It was a jarring description, considering the 49ers were drafting Smith with the No. 1 overall pick, paying him millions of dollars, and hoping he would be an immediate tonic to the flagging franchise.

As Harbaugh arrived six years later, the patience that Meyer urged in 2005 had been stretched to the breaking point. By the beginning of 2011, Smith had become like the Great Pumpkin in the Peanuts cartoons:

forever promised but never arriving. "I was robbed!" Sally Brown says in one strip after waiting up all night with Linus in the pumpkin patch for the tardy Great Pumpkin to appear. "You owe me restitution!" She sounded a lot like 49ers fans by the end of 2010 and 2011. They were tired of waiting. They were abandoning the pumpkin patch in droves.

Smith, too, had plenty of reason to leave. He had played for two defensive-minded head coaches who were clueless about managing a quarterback. His offensive coordinators either bolted after one season or were inept. Smith never could fully immerse himself in an offense the way Meyer said he needed to because he was having to learn a new one—first Mike McCarthy's, then Norv Turner's, then Jim Hostler's, then Mike Martz's, and so on—each offseason. The final straw seemed to be the Philadelphia Eagles game just three months before Harbaugh became the new head coach. Not only did Smith have to suffer the indignity of being upbraided on national television by a head coach, Mike Singletary, who had no idea how to make him better, but the fanbase also had turned on him. And this all came after he had tried to play with his right arm literally dangling out of its socket. Singletary's sideline diatribe gave the fans license to voice their displeasure with Smith, and during the game, they began chanting, "We want Carr! We want Carr!" That was the surname of Smith's backup, David Carr.

It got more uncomfortable than that. Smith's wife, Elizabeth, who was five months pregnant at the time, was in the stands with his parents and some of the other players' wives and girlfriends. A group of 10 or so fans, who obviously had been drinking heavily, were seated behind them and figured out who they were. The catcalls began early and grew more intense and more profane as Smith and the 49ers struggled early on in the game. When Singletary started jawing at the quarterback on the sideline, the group grew even nastier. "I'm pregnant, I'm watching Alex, and I can clearly see the distress on him," Elizabeth Smith recalled. "And at that point, I have tunnel vision on him. I want to see that he's okay.

And then the comments start up again: 'Oh, you gold digger, there goes your money! Those guys are gone! They're out of here!' They were making comments essentially about Alex's career being over. It was so vulgar and demeaning."

At that point, Erika Snyder, the wife of guard Adam Snyder, wheeled around and yelled something back to the group of men. "Then it was like things started flying at us," Elizabeth Smith said. "There was a beer bottle—a glass beer bottle—that definitely came in our direction. There was an older gentleman there, and he turned around and he did defend us. And then we were fearful for him because it was a group of guys that were probably between the ages of 20 and 30. And they were really intoxicated. They were looking for a fight."

After that episode it appeared as if a 49ers-Smith breakup was in the best interest of both parties. But there was a practical concern that most observers and certainly those howling for Smith's departure on social media and in newspapers' mailbag sections didn't grasp in the winter of 2011. The NFL was heading for a labor lockout, one that threatened to drag deep into the summer months. The draft would go on as scheduled, but free agency, which normally takes place in early March, wouldn't get underway until a new collective bargaining agreement was ratified. There would be no practices, no meetings, no interactions between players and coaches until there was a resolution, and no one had a good read on when that would be. It put a team like the 49ers—who not only had an incoming coaching staff, but also a head coach who was new to the NFL—at a decided disadvantage.

It meant that Harbaugh could draft a quarterback in April, but that there would be no offseason to teach him the offense and get him ready to play in the 2011 regular season. They could pick one up in free agency, but none of the quarterbacks available ever had played in the system that Harbaugh and Roman were running, and they would be starting from scratch when the lockout ended—whenever that would be. The 49ers were stuck. Unless, of course, they could force feed the offense into a quarterback's head before the lockout began. The 49ers quickly decided they would try to do so with Smith. "We were sprinting to get all this information to the players and to Alex Smith in particular," Roman said. "And there was a deadline. So we had to get it to him."

There were two problems with this plan. One was that Smith wasn't signed for the 2011 season. He was about to be a free agent. The 49ers could give him all the instruction they wanted until the lockout began in early March. After that, however, it was a leap of faith he wouldn't sign elsewhere. After that, he technically wasn't a 49er. The other issue was that the 49ers didn't know how good Smith would be. He'd never had a winning record, had suffered through a revolving door of offensive coordinators, and his confidence had been eroded by all the turnover, injuries, strife, and clumsiness that had surrounded him. How could it not be— given all that he had been through?

One of the first things Harbaugh did after he was hired was sit down and have a conversation with Smith. The new head coach wanted to get a read on the quarterback's character. "Did he want to be in the fire? Or did he want to wear the ball cap backward and back up somewhere?" Harbaugh said of the conversation. "And I really felt that he had the competitive drive, the [desire] to prove himself, him wanting to do it here. That's the thing that probably intrigued me the most: that character of wanting to come back and do it here in San Francisco, which is pretty rare, probably somewhere between rare and extinct. That's not just for football players. That's about anybody. And I thought we could really work with that character. To me that was special."

Harbaugh and his staff spent their first month not just pumping Smith full of Xs and Os information, but also pumping up his confidence both to his face and through the media. When a reporter asked Harbaugh if he was worried about how Smith, booed heavily the previous year, would react if that unhappy and unruly Candlestick chorus erupted in the upcoming year, the new head coach had a line ready. "Well, the question is: does he have baby deer skin or skin like an armadillo?" Harbaugh told *The Sacramento Bee* while a huge grin flashed across his face. "He's a tough son of a gun...I watched four really solid years of every snap that guy took: getting hit in the pocket, picking himself back up, playing under adversity, fierce competitor. I don't think [booing] will affect the guy."

Harbaugh was Smith's biggest fan. At least he was that season. Smith also had reason to stay. If he left San Francisco and joined a new team, he would begin behind any incumbent quarterbacks when the lockout finally ended. Sticking with the 49ers meant he would have a considerable head start on all challengers. His wife was from the Bay Area, his parents lived in San Diego, and he had become close with Joe Staley, Snyder, and other 49ers players. The duty-bound Smith also felt an obligation to finally lift the 49ers, the team that had once made him the first choice in the draft, back to the playoffs. He not only agreed to sign a contract once the lockout was over, he also agreed to become the team's de facto head coach and offensive coordinator during the long labor strife. Staley dubbed it "Camp Alex."

The Case of the White Mercedes

Shortly after the lockout began in March, the San Francisco 49ers players needed a place where they could work out near their South Bay Area homes. A number of them began showing up at nearby San Jose State University, which is only nine miles from 49ers team headquarters. Soon the team's veteran leaders began to realize that the longer the lockout dragged on, the worse it would be for the 49ers, who didn't even know which system they'd be running in the regular season. "We were excited about Harbaugh being our coach," offensive lineman Adam

Snyder said. "We had come off a bunch of losing seasons, the Singletary years. We wanted to work as hard as we could and be as prepared as possible. Alex and Justin [Smith] were the ringleaders. They were like, 'Hey, let's just do this on our own.' Otherwise, we were just going to be sitting around."

Justin Smith was in charge of organizing player workouts in the university's weight room. Anyone who peeked through the hedges at one of San Jose State's practice fields might have seen Justin Smith, Parys Haralson, and Ray McDonald amble by on all fours. That's because Justin Smith made everyone do bear crawls to stay in shape. "The couple years before then, our record didn't reflect it, but I thought we had a lot of talent, especially on the defensive side of the ball," Justin Smith said. "And with the lockout going on, I said, 'Shit, this is an opportunity.' A lot of guys would be doing their regular workouts, things like that. And we got together and we just humped it, running as hard as we could run. I mean, we took basically all the hardest workouts we could think of and did that and then did some more. I'm not saying that's what propelled us. We had tons of talent and stuff like that—probably mismanaged talent—and adding a coaching staff that would turn us loose a lot more, it kind of all just came together."

Smith was the oldest member of the defense and perhaps the most important member of that unit. "He was the guy motivating the others to play hard and to play above and beyond when they were on the field," defensive coordinator Vic Fangio said. "Those are things that coaches can't help with. Once they're out there, those 11 guys are on their own. To me that was one of the things that he brought to those three or four years when we were pretty successful. He had a lot of cache without trying. Guys looked up and respected him for the type of player he was then and had been for years. So he kind of carried a big stick with everybody."

Joe Staley was tasked with rounding up as many offensive linemen as possible. He, Snyder, Mike Iupati, Alex Boone, and center David Baas were among the regulars, and rookies Daniel Kilgore and Mike Person arrived after the draft. Alex Smith had by far the biggest job: gathering skill position players, installing the offense, and essentially running the team. The numbers began to swell during the spring until Smith held a more formal camp with more than two dozen players on hand in early June. "Alex would get the receivers, linemen, running backs—whoever was in town—and we would have chalk talks," Snyder said. "One of the equipment guys had given us a white board, and we had sessions where Alex was basically installing the offense. We'd go over that together, talk about it, go through calls and different formations. And then we would break off as an offensive line and sit in a classroom and go over our blocking stuff."

Smith wasn't supposed to have a playbook. After all, he was in no man's land at that point—a free agent in a league that hadn't yet had a free-agency signing period. Somehow a playbook ended up in his hands that spring. "Not that I can recall," Roman said when asked if the coaching staff was sneaking information to Smith during the lockout. "Isn't that what Ollie North said?"

Chase Beeler also mysteriously began showing up at the player-run practices at San Jose State. Beeler had been the center on Harbaugh's Stanford teams, which meant he knew Roman's offense as well as any player outside of quarterback Andrew Luck. Beeler had gone undrafted in April and (like Smith) would be part of the free-agency process whenever the lockout ended. He wasn't on any team at the time. The 49ers ended up bringing him in for training camp later that summer, but his true purpose in the spring was to help Smith teach the offensive system, especially to the offensive linemen. "We were bringing in this incredibly sophisticated system we had used with Andrew Luck that was sort of developed on the fly with Andrew Luck and those guys," Roman said. "And they were so smart. And everybody always said, 'You'll never be able to do it with this crew in San Francisco.' And it was a little bit of a scaled-down version. But we went all in on it from the start. It was a challenging system. Let's just say that. But it fed into Alex Smith's strengths. That was the beauty of it."

Smith, the guy fans couldn't wait to get rid of just a few months earlier, ended up being quarterback, offensive coordinator, travel coordinator, and big-pocket donor that summer. He came to a more formal arrangement with San Jose State officials for using the school's playing field, weight room, and meeting facility by making a substantial donation to the university's Spartan Foundation.

The quarterback did more than that, though it wasn't always appreciated. One of the team's draft picks that year was a receiver out of USC named Ronald Johnson. He was from Michigan and was living there when the 49ers started planning their player-run practices in late spring of 2011. Because no rookies had been paid at that point, Johnson needed help flying to San Jose so he could take part. Smith helped fly him to California. Then he went a step further. While he was in the Bay Area, Johnson lived at an extended-stay hotel in Santa Clara. He had no way to get back and forth to the practices at San Jose State. Smith could pick him up and drop him off each day, but then the rookie would then be stranded at the hotel. So Smith made an offer: would Johnson like to drive his wife's white Mercedes?

Elizabeth Smith had bought the car herself before she had married the No. 1 overall pick in the draft. She was proud of it. It symbolized her independence. But because the couple had just had their first child, she wasn't driving it at the time. And truth be told, she'd rather have her husband home to help out with the baby than commuting around the South Bay and dropping rookies off at their hotels. She was happy to lend Johnson her car for a few days.

Days, however, turned into weeks and then into months. Johnson didn't give the car back. Smith asked his wife to be patient; rookies still weren't getting paychecks and Johnson needed the car more than they did. But a month or so after the Mercedes was loaned, it became clear the Smiths' generosity was being abused. They started receiving tickets in the mail for traveling across the region's bridges without stopping and paying the toll. The tickets were $25 a piece, but they kept arriving in the mailbox and eventually totaled close to $1,000.

The story of the White C Class Mercedes doesn't end there. Despite taking part in the player-run practices and thus getting a leg up on his competition, Johnson wasn't very impressive when training camp finally opened in late July—nor was he any good during the preseason in August. As the 49ers trimmed their roster to 53 players in early September, Johnson was one of their cuts. When he became available, the receiver quickly was picked up by the Eagles and flew from the Bay Area to Philadelphia to join his new team.

The Smiths figured they'd finally get the car back. Alex texted Johnson to ask where it was but got no response. Two days later, Johnson texted back, writing that the car was parked in a corner of the extended-stay parking lot and that the keys were in the car. *Wait. The keys were in the car? Not at the front desk? Not left with the 49ers security staff just a couple of miles down the road?*

The Smiths put the baby in the second car and drove to the Santa Clara hotel. But there was no white Mercedes in the lot. They called Johnson, who wasn't interested in helping them figure out where it was. He wasn't with the 49ers anymore, and the just-beginning case of the missing Mercedes wasn't his problem. The Smiths soon filed a police report with the Santa Clara Police Department. Then they waited some more. Six months later, the mystery was solved. The couple's phone rang at 3:00 AM. Police had found the car at a Motel 6, another hotel in Santa Clara, and wanted them to come down and take a look.

They did so later that day along with a tow truck. The keys to the car were missing. When they popped the trunk, they found women's clothing, makeup, a scale, syringes, and a purse with identification inside it. It belonged to a woman well-known by police for working the hotels and motels in the area as a prostitute. Bleach had been poured over the backseat of the car. There also was a bullet hole in one of the back panels that police said had been fired from inside the vehicle. The car looked like it had been lived in. And worse, it also looked like it had been worked in. "This was my baby!" Elizabeth Smith said of the episode. "This was something I saved up for forever. I had taken such good care of her. And to find it like that—I mean, the backseat would be where I'd be putting my child. At that point, it was, 'Okay, we're done with this car.'"

Alex Smith never lost his focus during the car incident and he never grumbled to his teammates. He was the leader, and leaders don't complain. His theme that summer during Camp Alex was that the 49ers already were trailing the rest of the league and needed to sprint if they were to catch up. "We're behind the 8-ball," Smith said.

Following one of the player-led sessions, he spoke to the media. "I know what I installed and everything I basically threw at the wall," he said. "I don't know how much of it stuck to the wall. And I think that's going to be the test when these guys come back, whenever this thing ends. How much of it stuck?"

The 49ers would learn just how far behind they were when they played their preseason game in New Orleans against the Saints a month and a half later and when their offense sputtered badly on the road against the Cincinnati Bengals in Week Three of the regular season. But as Smith noted, the players got a broad foundation of the offense that summer. Perhaps more critical than that, they began interacting and bonding in a way no other team was doing at the time. Many of the rookies, who were flown in from all parts of the country, slept at the homes of veterans during Camp Alex. Staley, for example, had Kilgore, a fifth-round interior lineman from Appalachian State, and Person, a seventh-round tackle from Montana State, stay with him. On their first night together, the offensive line went to Hooters and had beer and wings.

For Kilgore that represented his first time in California and the first time he ever noticed Justin Smith. "I didn't know any of the defensive linemen," he said. "I just remember looking at Justin Smith and was like, 'Who the hell is that guy? That guy is a monster.' And I watched him in the weight room and I watched him run and I was like, 'Huh, he doesn't really look too athletic or anything.' I didn't know anything about the guy."

Kilgore would quickly find out who No. 94 was when training camp finally opened later that summer and the coaches called for him to go one on one against the veteran defensive lineman in a pass-blocking drill. "They wanted to break me in and give me that welcome-to-the-NFL moment," he said. "And that for sure happened with Justin Smith and me. Just from my experience, that guy was the hardest and just the best defensive tackle I had to go against. And that was just in practice."

Not everyone showed up or was enthusiastic about the practices at San Jose State. When receiver Michael Crabtree reluctantly arrived for one of the sessions, he sniffed at the uncertainty of the situation, saying, "I wish I could tell you who is going to be the quarterback. I don't know."

Everyone else, however, said it was clear who was in charge. That was one of the benefits of Camp Alex. Getting a taste of the offense was one thing. Setting the tone for the rest of the season was far more important. "The success we had that year—it all started with Alex having those meetings, holding those workouts, working with the receivers, the young guys, and kind of taking the whole team under his wing," Kilgore said. "You could tell what kind of leader Alex Smith was and the type of guy he was. For a guy to do that all on his own, pay for it, want the guys to work out together, that's the guy I wanted to go to battle for."

Snyder agreed. "Yeah, I definitely think that that had something to do with how the season turned out," he said. "Because when you trust somebody, when you spend time with somebody off the field in situations like that, you build trust, you build bonding. The time that we were able to spend outside the football facility doing football stuff, doing non-football stuff, was a huge factor, I think, for the season."

CHAPTER 4
NEXT STOP, YOUNGSTOWN

While the offensive coaches tried to be as productive as possible during the lockout—watching film of their new pupils, scouting upcoming opponents, perhaps sneaking information to Alex Smith—the team's defensive coordinator played it cool. Vic Fangio, who was 52 at the time, had been running NFL defenses since 1995. One of the things he'd learned when it came to joining a new squad: it made no sense to pore over game film of the players he inherited. After all, he didn't know exactly what their assignments and responsibilities had been under the previous defensive coordinator. How could he judge a player who was operating in someone else's defense? Lockout or not, Fangio would decide on starters, backups, who should play which position—even the style of defense he would run—only after he watched his new players in the flesh.

The sole exception he made shortly after joining the San Francisco 49ers was defensive lineman Ray McDonald. He had been a third-round pick four years earlier but never had risen to the status of full-time starter. He was heading toward free agency in 2011, and the 49ers had a chance to sign him to a new contract before the lockout began. General manager Trent Baalke asked Fangio to watch film of McDonald to see if he thought he'd be worth a contract. The coordinator liked what he saw. "Our system benefited him, and I think at that point in his career, he was ready to play," Fangio said. "I also think Justin [Smith] had a real positive effect on him."

McDonald made an immediate impact, recording six tackles in the opening game against the Seattle Seahawks in 2011, including three hits—and one sack—on quarterback Tarvaris Jackson. McDonald became a starter that year, finishing with a career-high five-and-a-half sacks and forcing two fumbles. Linebacker NaVorro Bowman, who had been a third-round pick a year earlier, never had been a full-time starter in San Francisco until Fangio arrived. Neither had outside linebacker Ahmad

Brooks or cornerback Tarell Brown. All of them became regulars on the 2011 unit, and one of them, Bowman, became a star.

Fangio was methodical even after the lockout ended in late July. That also marked the start of free agency, and teams scrambled to sign the top names on the market. Agents slept in their offices in order to handle the round-the-clock rush. Fangio, however, remained patient. He first wanted to observe his incumbent players in action before the 49ers made any additions in free agency. "After the first week or so, once we were working with the guys, it didn't feel like we were good enough in the secondary," he said. "And I can remember coming off the practice field in training camp and Baalke walking up and saying, 'We need to take a quick look here at Donte Whitner.' And I think he said, 'We've got about a half hour to decide, or he's going to go to Cincinnati.' So I watched about 25 minutes of tape on Donte. And Baalke said it was for reasonable money. I thought he was better than what we were working with, and we signed him."

Whitner went on to start 15 games that season, record 62 tackles, haul in two interceptions, and deliver one of the most ferocious, iconic hits in franchise history. In addition to having no offseason with the 49ers, he also didn't sign with the team until August 4, 10 days after NFL owners and players announced the lockout had been lifted. By that point the 49ers were shopping in the free-agency bargain bin. At cornerback they landed Carlos Rogers, a former first-round pick with the Washington Redskins, who never had lived up to his draft billing there. Rogers' biggest issue: unreliable hands. He only had eight interceptions in six seasons with the Redskins and had become infamous for allowing several would-be takeaways to slip through his fingers. Under Fangio and defensive backs coach Ed Donatell, he had six interceptions in his first season with San Francisco.

The last member of the defense to arrive was safety Dashon Goldson. He didn't sign until August 8, four days before the team's first preseason game. Unlike Whitner and Rogers, Goldson not only had been a member of the 49ers, but he also had started for the team. But he felt he deserved a richer contract, and when he didn't get it from San Francisco, he hit the open market in search of a fat, free-agent deal. "Everybody in that building thought it was time for him to move on," Fangio said. "He had to some degree—and I don't remember why—worn out his welcome there. And he thought he could get pretty good money on the free-agent market. And then, I don't know, maybe 10 days into free agency, he's still not signed."

Baalke again approached Fangio after practice and said the 49ers could bring back Goldson on a one-year deal. Did the defensive coordinator want him? "I had never watched him before, but I said, 'What the hell? Let's go. Let's sign him,'" Fangio said. "For the time he was here, he was as good a safety as there was in football. Those three signings happened a week to 10 days after we started camp. And that's 75 percent of your secondary when you've got four defensive backs out there."

The three free agents were joined by Brown, a first-year starter, and Chris Culliver, a rookie the 49ers had drafted in the third round. None had played together before, and most had been thrown in at the last minute. The unit, however, would end the season with 19 interceptions in the regular season and with two more—Goldson's and Brown's interceptions of New Orleans Saints quarterback Drew Brees—in the playoffs. Goldson and Rogers would make the Pro Bowl that season, and Whitner would be voted in the following year. None had ever been Pro Bowlers previously. But they played cohesively and with obvious chemistry. "You would have thought we played together for a while," Rogers said. "But that was our first year."

In the summer of 2011, of course, Fangio didn't know how good the secondary would be. He wasn't sure what he had but was intent on finding out. Instead of simplifying the defense to accommodate a host of new players and to account for the lost offseason, Fangio did the opposite.

He put them into all sorts of configurations during training camp practices. "I took the attitude that we need to expose them to everything we might want to do because in case we need it—we need to have some background in it," Fangio said. "Plus, we needed to know what fit them. So we exposed them to a lot in training camp, and then by Week Three or Four of the regular season, I kind of figured out what's best for those guys."

Rogers recalled that Fangio did throw a lot of defensive looks at his players in training camp. But everyone, especially the members of the secondary, was smart enough to pick it up and, more importantly, able to retain everything they experimented with that summer. That proved to be important when Fangio wanted to make adjustments for specific opponents during the regular season. "It allowed us to go into games against different offenses and say, 'Okay, y'all remember when we did this in the summer? We're going to put this in this week,'" Rogers said. "So once the season went on, those defenses came up again, and when they did, it was easy for us to grasp and easy for him to coach. We had gone over so much stuff in training camp, it was easy to pick up. And sometimes it wouldn't come up until, say, Week 6."

The camaraderie, the coaching—there was something to the brew the 49ers quickly threw together in the summer of 2011. "I played on some good, talented teams," Rogers said. "The talent in Washington with Shawn Springs, Smoot, Ryan Clark, LaRon Landry—we had some talent in Washington. But we didn't play as good as we played in San Fran. It was the best defense I played on. It's proven—and with guys that didn't even know each other."

Stomped in the Superdome

One of the last free agents the San Francisco 49ers ended up signing in the summer of 2011 was center Jonathan Goodwin. He wasn't easy to land. Goodwin had been the starting center on the New Orleans Saints' Super Bowl-winning team in 2009. New Orleans and the Superdome had been battered and beaten down by Hurricane Katrina four years earlier. The Saints, a franchise that never had won a title and that was a paper bag punch line through much of its existence, helped lift the sunken city from its grief during a storybook playoff run. Goodwin was part of that. He had made powerful, lifelong bonds in the locker room and in the community. New Orleans—its people, its culture, its resilience—had seeped into his bloodstream. He didn't want to leave. But the Saints and general manager Mickey Loomis didn't want to pay him.

So he took a free-agent visit to Santa Clara, California, in early August and had dinner with Jim Harbaugh and Greg Roman. The two 49ers coaches left the dinner thinking they had Goodwin on board. Goodwin, who played at Michigan and who called the shots for the Saints' sophisticated run-blocking schemes, was known for his smarts. It's what allowed him to be an NFL center for 13 seasons. But he's also exceedingly soulful and sensitive. And those two facets—his brain and his heart—went to war after he agreed to join the 49ers. "I went back to the hotel and I went to sleep," Goodwin said. "And I woke up at 4 or 5 in the morning in a panic. I was like, 'I can't do this!' So I called my agent. He called Coach Harbaugh and Trent Baalke. They come to the hotel and they try to talk me out of leaving. They just told me to keep thinking about it. So I went back up to my room and thought about it, but I couldn't convince myself. I actually told my wife, 'No, I can't do it. I want to go back to New Orleans.'"

So Goodwin hopped in a cab and went to the airport. He was about to board his plane back to New Orleans when his agent called: the 49ers had just increased their offer on a three-year deal. Was he sure he wanted to leave the Bay Area without signing? "Once again I changed my mind, and Trent Baalke came and picked me up from the airport, and I ended up signing a contract and becoming a 49er," he said. "I still remember to this day, in my first o-line meeting, I was still kind of sad because I had built such a close relationship with guys in New Orleans, especially all my linemates and things like that. I guess it took some time for me to get over the love that I had for New Orleans and wanting to be a Saint."

Nine days after signing with the 49ers, Goodwin and his new teammates began the 2011 preseason in—where else?—the New Orleans Superdome. The first exhibition game of the year is supposed to be a vanilla affair. Teams insert their starters for a series or two, run their most basic offensive concepts, and play a staid, standard style on defense. The main objective is to emerge without any major injuries. Given that all of the NFL teams had only been practicing for a little more than a week because of the lockout, 2011's preseason openers were expected to be even more mundane than normal.

This one wasn't.

The Saints played as if they were out for blood, sending all-out blitzes on nearly every passing down. Because of the lockout, it was the first time Roman's offense had lined up in a game situation. Two of his offensive linemen, left guard Mike Iupati and right tackle Anthony Davis, were entering their second seasons. They clearly weren't ready for what Saints defensive coordinator Gregg Williams had in store. "It was our first game under Harbaugh, and I remember it just being a shitshow," tackle Joe Staley said. "You go into preseason games, especially the first preseason game, and usually it's just, like, getting back to football."

"Everybody and their brother was basically saying, 'Hey, these guys weren't prepared,'" Roman said. "That was kind of the spin on it. 'Man, the 49ers' new coaching staff, boy, they got schooled. They sure weren't prepared.'"

Though it wasn't made public until later in 2011, Williams and the Saints were being investigated for what became known as Bountygate, a scandal in which the Saints defensive players were given bonuses for injuring opposing players. The league found that Williams initiated the program when he arrived in New Orleans in 2009 as a way to spark an aggressive mentality with his unit. For example, players earned $1,000 for what they called "cart-offs"— instances, in which an opponent suffered an injury so severe he had to be removed by a cart or a stretcher. A player also could earn a $1,500 bonus for a knockout, in which an offensive opponent couldn't return for the rest of the game.

That was the type of marauding attitude the Saints defense brought into the 2011 preseason opener. Alex Smith was flung to the turf on his first pass attempt and sacked on his second by a crushing blind-side hit by safety Roman Harper that struck the quarterback squarely in the center of his back and jarred the ball loose. Williams' defense sacked Smith and his backup, Colin Kaepernick, six times in the first half alone and knocked them down another four times. "I didn't even have a mouthpiece in that game," Smith said. "I remember thinking, *I'm going to get rid of the ball, throw a few completions, move the chains, and I'll be off the field before you know it.* And I think we got cover zero and overload pressures on an absurd number of snaps. I think when we looked back, it was like 14 out of 18 snaps or something."

"He was bringing corner blitzes and everything," Goodwin said. "Being a guy that had been around Gregg Williams a lot—on road trips I sat like two rows behind him on the bus—so I knew what kind of coach he was. He was an aggressive coach. But from my memory of being with him, I never remembered him blitzing that way in a first preseason game, especially after the lockout and things like that."

After the game some speculated that because the lockout had wiped away so many offseason practices, Williams simply wanted to jump-start his defense with an ultra-aggressive performance to begin the preseason. Later, however, another explanation emerged.

Prior to a preseason game, it's common practice for the two head coaches to talk to one another and hash out some ground rules—for example, the types of blitzes, if any, that might be used—for the upcoming contest. Apparently, Saints head coach Sean Payton called Harbaugh before their teams' meeting, but Harbaugh never called him back. In Payton's mind this was a serious diss and breach of etiquette by Harbaugh, a rookie NFL coach.

Zach Strief, who was then the Saints right tackle and a close friend of Goodwin, said he remembers being puzzled by all the blitzing during the game and learning the root of it a few days afterward. "The way I remember it being explained to me is: Jim Harbaugh refused to accept the phone call. And he refused to accept any rules," he said. "And I think eventually Sean went back and said, 'He doesn't want to talk. So there's no rules. Do whatever you want.' And Gregg's response was, 'Awesome. I'm going to hit the quarterback on every play' because that's what Gregg does."

Jeff Duncan, a longtime New Orleans sports columnist, who was writing for *The Times-Picayune* at the time, heard the same thing. "Gregg Williams probably has the black hat on that, but I think he was just following orders," Duncan said. "I know Gregg pretty well, and he's definitely a rare personality and an aggressive personality. But that even by his standards is a little out of character. And I just can't see him doing that. I've never seen him do it any other time."

For his part Harbaugh never acknowledged rejecting Payton's phone call or having a beef with the Saints head coach, who is just as fiery and pugnacious as he is. But he also didn't deny that it happened. Harbaugh, a history buff who is especially interested in and well-versed about World

War II, loved to paint scenarios in which his noble band of brothers was pitted against a nefarious enemy force.

In Harbaugh-speak, players and colleagues were "trusted agents." Anyone on the outside was suspicious, a potential threat. He was stingy with information to reporters because he said he worried that anything that was written about his team was being poured over by enemy combatants. The story of the unreturned phone call and the aggressive, unfair way Payton, Williams, and the Saints reacted to it slid perfectly into that very Harbaugh-ian psychology. "There was a malicious intent behind it," Staley said of the Saints' surprising gameplan. "And that was kind of Harbaugh's deal, too. Even if there wasn't, he got you to believe that there was. That was his motivational tactic. He was going to always play that everybody-hates-you kind of card. He got the guys to really buy into all that stuff."

This time, however, Harbaugh didn't need to cajole the 49ers into hating the Saints. The players and coaching staff all felt the same way as they trudged off the Superdome field following a humbling 24–3 loss. "Oh, everybody was definitely a little pissed off," Alex Smith said. "They had showed us up. You know, it was a dickhead thing to do. You heard this whole thing, like we didn't exactly kiss the ring or something."

"I'll never forget walking out of the locker room after that first game," Roman said. "We had just gotten blitzed into the Stone Age. And I remember telling Joe Staley: 'We'll get these guys in the playoffs. Don't worry.' And I kind of believed it, too. I don't know if he did at the time."

His words ended up being prophetic.

"There was something personal going on," Goodwin said. 'I don't know what. But I definitely think there was something personal there. Also, I'm sure they never thought they would see us again that season."

The Strip

When the regular season kicked off on September 11, the offense had improved. Slightly. The San Francisco 49ers won Jim Harbaugh's debut, a game against his one-time college head-coaching rival, Pete Carroll. But the offense gained a paltry 209 yards in the contest and pulled away from the Seattle Seahawks only because speedy return man Ted Ginn Jr. scored a pair of touchdowns on special teams in the fourth quarter.

The 49ers cobbled together only 206 yards the following week in a loss to the Dallas Cowboys and then went on the road to face the Cincinnati Bengals. Cincinnati fans thought the contest would be so dismal they didn't buy enough tickets, and the game was blacked out on local television. It was the smallest crowd for a Bengals home opener in 30 years. The city of Cincinnati was wise to look away. The score was 3–0 Bengals at halftime. Neither team had even close to 100 passing yards. And the 49ers and Bengals combined for nine punts before the break. "I remember coming down the elevator at halftime and saying to myself: *that might be the worst half of football I've ever seen,*" Roman said. "I don't know what the right word is, but I was thirsting for something—anything—at all. That's where we were at that time."

Roman had two plays he was saving for just the right moment, a throw back to tight end Vernon Davis and a bounce run for rookie tailback Kendall Hunter. Those were the team's most electric weapons on offense, the only players who could manufacture a spark. The trick was getting them in space at just the right moment. At the start of the fourth quarter, the 49ers were trailing 6–3, and Roman had no choice but to unveil both plays. Each worked.

Hunter gained 11 yards on his carry. Then at the Cincinnati 27-yard line, Roman called the play for Davis. Alex Smith faked a handoff and rolled to his right. Then he turned and fired the ball in the opposite direction to Davis, who was by himself and ran to the Bengals 7-yard line. Two plays later Hunter scampered into the end zone for the only touchdown of the day. The 49ers went on to win 13–8, but the celebration was muted. No one was optimistic. Starting running back Frank Gore had badly sprained his ankle in the second half. The 49ers essentially had one good drive. And the offensive players felt they had let down their defensive counterparts, who had intercepted rookie Andy Dalton twice and left him with an ugly 40.8 passer rating. "Our defense won that game," offensive tackle Joe Staley said. "Our offense was absolute trash."

There was one more thing to be down about as the team left the visiting locker room in Cincinnati: instead of heading home to the Bay Area, the 49ers would be spending the week in Youngstown, Ohio. It's the one-time steel mill town where former owner Eddie DeBartolo, Jr. and his sister, Denise, are from. And it's where the de facto owner of the team, Jed York, grew up as well. The family had an excellent relationship with Youngstown State, and the 49ers figured it would be a perfect spot to prepare for the upcoming game in Philadelphia. Instead of flying all the way back to San Jose and then heading back to the East Coast, they stayed in Northeastern Ohio for a week and shaved off 4,100 miles of air travel.

The only issue from the players' perspective: there's not much to do in Youngstown. There's no thriving downtown, no fancy hotels. The 49ers stayed at a Holiday Inn in nearby Boardman, Ohio, where the nightlife activity mainly consisted of walking across the street to Handel's Ice Cream shop and ordering two scoops of coconut almond fudge ripple.

There were two notable ripples to the team that week. The first was that Harbaugh held a walk-through practice in the sprawling parking lot next to the hotel. In typical Harbaugh fashion, he had a phalanx of buses form a circle around the session just in case any Philadelphia Eagles spies had infiltrated the Holiday Inn staff and were trying to peek in. The cloak-and-dagger head coach was in heaven. "That big slab of cement in the parking lot even had lines and tall trees around it. It was very private there," he gleefully exclaimed after the session. "That was one of the finer walk-through spots I've been associated with."

The other event was a bit more exciting. During one of the meal services, Adam Snyder, who at that point in the season had been a reserve guard, got in trouble in the dining area at the Holiday Inn. "We had just gotten to the hotel and we were starving," Daniel Kilgore said.

"And Adam started choking."

"We were eating steak at the table and cutting it up, and all of a sudden, he starts gagging, making all these choking sounds," Staley said. "And he stumbles over to the trash can."

"It's happened before where it just goes down the wrong pipe," Snyder said. "And panic sets in real quick. And when you're panicking, you're not breathing. There was something just lodged in my throat. I couldn't even drink water."

His teammates stood to help him, but someone else was much faster on his feet. The way Staley describes it, Harbaugh was on the other side of the room when he saw his player in distress. The head coach was off in a flash, barreling toward Snyder like a fullback through the line of scrimmage, pushing through groups of people and throwing aside tables and chairs along the way. Then he began beating on the 300-pound offensive lineman's back. "And it's like—*boom*—he punches him in the back so hard you could hear it," Staley said.

Said Snyder: "Yeah, Harbaugh gave my ass the Heimlich. He was smacking the heck out of me, just smashing my back. At one point he picked me up and it was like—*blewp*—it went down. And it was, 'Oh my God! He just saved my life!'"

Anyone who's met Harbaugh can envision him reacting that way. He is the protagonist in any room he is in. But upsetting chairs as he cut a path toward a choking victim? That has to be a bit of hyperbole, right? "No, that's exactly how it happened," Snyder said. "The thing with Coach Harbaugh is that everything he does is a 1,000 percent. And he's like that 24/7. It's just who he is. So if he sees one of his players choking, he is making his way over there as quickly as possible, no doubt about it."

"Oh yeah, that's how it happened," Kilgore confirmed. "He saw it happening from across the room. It was a big conference room. And he pushed through guys to get to Adam and then he literally saved his life. Like, Adam was scared. And we were wondering, *what's wrong with this guy?* And Harbaugh comes over and just reacts. It was pretty impressive. Then he just went back to his conversation."

Otherwise, there wasn't much action at the Holiday Inn, which, of course, pleased the coaching staff, which at that point still was trying to figure out the best offensive and defensive schemes to use that season. The 49ers very much remained a work in progress as the month of September drew to a close. "Any time a team can spend time together, good things come of it," Vic Fangio said. "We had training camp at our own facility, and that's not the same as going away for training camp. Because when guys had free time in training camp, they would go home. Whereas when you have free time in Youngstown, Ohio, you're not doing anything. You're staying with your guys. I remember guys coming downstairs at night looking for something to do, looking for some tape to watch because they had nothing else to do. I was more than happy to help them out."

The players didn't exactly appreciate the bond that was being forged in the old steel mill town—at least not at the time. It mostly seemed like a tedious week. Gore didn't practice at all, gloomily confiding in teammates that he didn't think he would play against Philadelphia. His sprained ankle was just too sore. Toward the end of the week in Ohio, reporters spoke with an ornery Staley, who was the de facto captain of the offensive line.

Smith had been sacked 11 times in the last two games—not to mention the bombardment he had suffered at the New Orleans Saints in the preseason opener. The 49ers had rushed for only 50 yards against Cincinnati, and Gore had been held under 60 yards rushing in every game thus far. Staley was asked what was going on with the offensive line. "I was super pissed that I had to talk to the media," Staley said. "You guys were asking questions like, 'What do you have to do better?' We played like absolute shit on the o-line the week before against Cincinnati. We got reamed. [Then-offensive line coach Mike] Solari would never yell at us. But Solari would have these moods where you felt so ashamed of what you did. He was the ultimate disappointed dad. At that point in my life, I was more upset at disappointing Solari than I was disappointing my own dad. He had a way of just making you feel like absolute shit. That night we had one of those meetings and we all went to bed angry. And then in the morning, I had to talk to the media."

At one point in the interview about him and his fellow offensive lineman, Staley blurted out, "Contrary to what everybody believes, we don't suck." The next day newspaper editors in Northern California had boiled it down to this headline: 49ers' Staley: "We don't suck." "In my mind, it wasn't a rallying cry or anything like that," Staley said. "I was just in such a bad mood that day. I just wanted to go to practice."

His quote seemed destined to be resurrected as the game against the Eagles began the following Sunday. Philadelphia had assembled a virtual All-Star squad before the season, a group that included cornerbacks Nnamdi Asomugha and Dominique Rodgers-Cromartie, quarterbacks Michael Vick and Vince Young, defensive end Jason Babin, and running backs LeSean McCoy and Ronnie Brown. The roster included 10 players with 25 Pro Bowl appearances among them. It was nicknamed the "Dream Team." They were the darlings of the NFL at the start of the season.

And against the 49ers, the Eagles played like they were elite, roaring out to a 20–3 lead at halftime. San Francisco's offense again stumbled. Smith had only 90 passing yards at the break. He had been sacked two times and fumbled once. The offensive line hadn't gotten any better, and the defense, which had carried the 49ers through the first three weeks, was wobbling as well. Inside the visiting locker room, no one panicked. The defensive coaches told their players the 49ers would start scoring points. The offensive coaches assured their pupils the defense would slow the Eagles, who had already accumulated 293 yards in the first half. To put that in perspective, a week earlier the Bengals had 228 yards…total. "I think it was Justin [Smith] who said, 'Okay, it's time to pull this game out of our ass. We have good players, we have a good team, we have good coaching,'" Snyder said. "'We've got to go. It's on us now. We've got to go.' And I think it just started to click."

Said Smith: "It was just a feeling that we knew we were pretty damn good. And it didn't matter that we were on the road or Philly being a pretty damn good team. The mentality was starting to change, especially on the defensive side of the ball. We knew we could make a big play—a pick or a strip or something we felt could happen at any time. I mean, you looked around that roster, and guys were just flying around, having fun, kicking some ass."

The 49ers were still trying new things on offense at that point in the season. Snyder, for example, was inserted at right guard in place of Chilo Rachal to start the game. Roman also had changed how he called the plays. Instead of sending one play call into Alex Smith's headset, he started sending in three. It was up to Smith to decide which of the three plays to choose, based on what he was seeing from the defense. "Alex was a smart guy," Snyder said. "And he'd been in so many offenses—he'd been in, like seven offenses—that they were tapping into his ability to read defenses, to be able to handle the pressure of making the right call.

Justin Smith forces a fumble against the Philadelphia Eagles in 2011, which changed the course of the game and the 49ers' season. (Terrell Lloyd / San Francisco 49ers)

I don't know how many other teams have done something like that. I know for sure we never did. Obviously, there are ways to kill and get out of plays. But no team that I'd been around was doing three-layered play calls. I'd never even heard of it."

At halftime Roman decided the best way to beat the Eagles was to batter them. He called trap plays. He'd send a tight end in motion only to bring him back to the line of scrimmage and crack down on the Eagles interior lineman. He had Mike Iupati, who at 6'5", 331 pounds was the biggest of all the 49ers players, pull from his left guard spot, come around the corner, and plow into the hole. Most of all, he had Gore at his disposal in the game.

The running back had surprised Harbaugh and Roman by insisting he could play. Gore, who had come back from two major knee operations and who loved playing football more than anything in the world, had decided he couldn't stand to watch from the sideline. The coaches knew his confidence wasn't merely fool's courage when Gore ripped off a 40-yard run on his first carry. Heading into the game, Harbaugh had all but written Gore's name on the inactive list. "After that game I never doubted Frank Gore again," he'd say afterward.

Said Roman: "I was kind of shocked that he was gonna play. And then he took the first run for 40 yards. It was a trap…And he popped the trap and, as only Frank could do back then, he got up on the safety and broke the safety's ankles and made him miss."

The Eagles opened the second half with a field goal that made the score 23–3. After that the 49ers began to throw their weight around. On their second drive, Smith hit Josh Morgan with a short pass over the middle, and the receiver weaved his way through the Philadelphia secondary for a 30-yard touchdown. The next time the 49ers had the ball, Smith connected with the other starting wideout, Michael Crabtree, for 38 yards and then found Davis for a nine-yard score. Suddenly, it was 23–17 heading into the fourth quarter.

The Eagles seemed to steady themselves with an 11-play drive to San Francisco's 15-yard line that burned more than five minutes from the clock. Their field goal try, however, spun wide right. The 49ers took advantage with a drive of their own, one that featured another long run from Gore, which went up the middle for 25 yards. Six plays later Gore bounced to his right for a 12-yard score that gave the 49ers their first lead of the day.

A photo of the touchdown shows Gore reaching the ball across the goal line with all five 49ers offensive linemen and fullback Bruce Miller behind him, and their arms are raised in triumph. It was a fitting image for a game in which the 49ers finally were able to not just move the ball, but also move their opponents. They finished with 164 rushing yards, and 127 of them came from Gore, the guy who nobody thought would play. "That's who Frank Gore is," Snyder said. "He's not going to leave the game. If there's any chance to play, he's playing. That's just classic Frank Gore."

The contest, however, wasn't over. There still was a little more than three minutes to play, the Eagles had two timeouts, and the 49ers defense hadn't been able to clamp down on Vick and the Philadelphia offense, which finished with 513 yards on the afternoon. It was the most yards the defense would allow all season, including in the playoffs.

The 49ers didn't put up much resistance on the Eagles' final drive either. Philadelphia took over at its 20-yard line and—thanks in part to two offsides penalties on Ahmad Brooks—quickly moved the ball to midfield. When Vick tossed a short pass to receiver Jeremy Maclin, it seemed as if the 49ers' lead would be short-lived. There were no 49ers around him, and he ran so far down field that the Eagles would, at the very least, be left with a field-goal try to retake the lead.

An unlikely defender made sure that didn't happen. Justin Smith, who had led the defense through the offseason workouts at San Jose and who had delivered the calm but forceful message to the locker room at halftime, took off from his defensive end position when the ball left Vick's hand. Smith was in his 11th season at the time and weighed close to 300 pounds. He already had played 70 snaps in the contest and was at the end of the two-game road trip in the Eastern time zone. When Maclin, nine years younger and 100 pounds lighter, made the catch at the 50-yard line, Smith was six yards behind him.

Seventeen yards later he had caught up to the ball carrier and, as Smith pounced on Maclin from behind, he punched his left hand—the white tape on his fingers had turned a grimy brown at that point—toward the football. It popped loose at the 31-yard line and began rolling toward the 49ers sideline. If an Eagles player grabbed it or if the ball touched the white boundary marker, Philadelphia would retain possession. At first every 49ers player on the sideline began screaming, "Get the ball! Get the ball!" Then the cries quickly changed to "Stay in bounds! Stay in bounds!" Safety Dashon Goldson dove and cradled it in one motion mere inches from the sideline. The Eagles drive—miraculously—had been halted, and Smith was mobbed by delirious teammates. "You stick your arm through there and hope the ball's there," the defensive lineman said afterward. "It's a drill you work on every day. It kind of becomes repetition. Like I said, you're really not trying to get the tackle. You're trying to get the ball out. And luckily enough, it was there."

"The pursuit, the hustle he showed, I mean, that's where the story is to me," Harbaugh said.

Fangio, who thought he'd seen everything by that point in his career, was the most impressed observer of all. "I tried to get that nicknamed, 'The Strip' and get it equal billing with 'The Catch,'" he said. "It didn't stick."

Still, there was 2:06 remaining, and the Eagles had one more timeout to burn. The rest of the game read like a play-by-play sheet from the 1960s: Gore up the middle for four yards, Gore right end for eight yards, Gore up the middle for five yards. The 49ers wore out an Eagles defense that knew exactly what was coming and thus ran out the clock. "You'll never see another two-minute drive like it in the NFL," Roman said. "We ran it darn near every play. That never happens. We had seven offensive linemen in the game. We had as many offensive linemen on the field as humanly possible."

It's hard to overstate the importance of the win. It marked the first time the 49ers had won back-to-back road games in a decade. It helped forge the team's identity—a might-is-right squad that outmuscles opponents at the line of scrimmage and would outlast them at the end of games. "Our entire thing on offense at that time was that we were going to out-physical you," Staley said. "That was our mentality."

Most of all it confirmed what the players felt when Harbaugh and his staff took over. Mike Nolan and Mike Singletary had tried to build bullying offensive lines over the years but couldn't do much with them.

Harbaugh essentially inherited a pro version of the power-running teams he had at Stanford. He, Roman, and the 49ers roster were perfect matches. It just took a few games to get going. The win in Philadelphia was a confidence boost for the 49ers and a wake-up call for the rest of the league. The long-dormant franchise was awake again.

An Earthquake of a Handshake

The San Francisco 49ers returned to the Bay Area with newfound assurance. Before the next game against the Tampa Bay Buccaneers, Alex Smith approached Greg Roman, who had been conservative with his new quarterback to start the season. "Alex Smith came to me and said, 'I really want to be more aggressive throwing the ball down the field when we get to the 30-yard line or around there,'" Roman said. "And I said, 'Okay, what do you want to run?' And he gave me a play."

Smith didn't have to wait long to use it. On their first possession, he and the 49ers drove to the Tampa Bay 26-yard line. From there Smith dropped back and hit the team's other tight end, Delanie Walker, on a deep pass down the right side of the field for a touchdown. Smith went on on to throw three touchdowns in the game as the 49ers blew out the Buccaneers 48–3. "That was a big step for him and our relationship," Roman said of him and Smith. "I had kind of been protecting him. And he asked for [the play]. It came up, and he nailed it. So that was huge for him as a leader and for his confidence. That was really big for him."

The win set up the next big challenge for the suddenly surging 49ers: a road game against the Detroit Lions. At that point San Francisco had won three straight games, a nice little streak. The Lions were even hotter. They hadn't lost a game since December 5, 2010. They had a fiery, hard-nosed head coach in Jim Schwartz and suddenly had a wild, rowdy atmosphere in sold-out Ford Field. National writers from *The Sporting News* and *The New York Times* showed up for the game between two upstart teams. Those reporters would have plenty to write about. "It was so loud," Roman said. "That place was rolling. That's what they envisioned in Detroit: an indoor stadium, all that crowd noise. It was a lot like Seattle."

There also was plenty of energy coming from the two head coaches. Jim Harbaugh and Schwartz had met earlier that year. The ongoing lockout was all anyone could talk about at that time, and according to a 49ers team official, Schwartz made a comment to Harbaugh that a long work stoppage would be particularly damaging to a team like the 49ers. This was true. A team with a new coaching staff, one that was overhauling a big portion of its roster, would have a limited amount of time to evaluate talent and teach new offensive and defensive systems and was at a disadvantage. Schwartz, however, may have shown a little too much glee in pointing that out. It was as if the Lions head coach was sticking it to Harbaugh. Schwartz acted like a yapper, a talker, a blowhard. In other words, he wasn't a Harbaugh type of guy.

There also was an incident in the first quarter of the game. After a 16-yard touchdown from Lions quarterback Matthew Stafford to tight end Brandon Pettigrew put Detroit ahead 10–0, Harbaugh decided he wanted to review the score and threw his red challenge flag. The officials responded by tossing a yellow handkerchief toward Harbaugh. All scoring plays are automatically reviewed, and it was a 15-yard penalty to challenge such a play. It was a mistake by the first-time NFL head coach.

He and the 49ers were thoroughly discombobulated at that moment. Harbaugh's penalty already was the seventh one they'd committed inside Detroit's noisy stadium, and there was still nearly five minutes to go in the opening quarter. The offense was flustered. And Schwartz again seemed to react to Harbaugh's obstacles with unbridled joy. Television cameras caught him yelling across the field during the 49ers coach's ill-fated challenge: "Know the fucking rules, Harbaugh!" That it was shown in slow motion only emphasized the animus coming from the Lions head coach.

It was then that the 49ers sprung to life. His ankle now fully recovered, Frank Gore broke free up the middle for a 47-yard gain to the Detroit 1-yard line. From there Roman sent in the team's heavy jumbo package, one that featured an extra offensive lineman, Alex Boone, and a 330-pound nose tackle moonlighting as a fullback, Isaac Sopoaga. It wasn't merely a gimmicky goal-line look; Roman used it throughout the game. Two plays after his long run, Gore crashed into the end zone for the 49ers' first score of the day.

Schwartz had been a former defensive coordinator, and the Lions' Ndamukong Suh was perhaps the best defensive tackle in the league at the time. The Detroit defensive line also included first-round pick Nick Fairley and well-regarded defensive ends Kyle Vanden Bosch and Cliff Avril. That defensive line gave Detroit its identity, and the 49ers attacked the heart of it. "I remember we schemed to play Ndamukong Suh," lineman Adam Snyder said. "We were hitting him from every angle. We had H-backs hitting him. We trapped him. We had all sorts of things in the gameplan to attack what they did best, which was their d-line."

After Gore's touchdown Aldon Smith sacked Stafford in the end zone for a safety. Just before the half, David Akers nailed a 55-yard field goal, his longest of the season. The 49ers went into the locker room leading 12–10, and suddenly Schwartz wasn't so giddy.

The teams traded field goals in the third quarter. Early in the fourth quarter, the Lions moved ahead again 19–15, following a five-yard pass from Stafford to Nate Burleson. If the 49ers were to win their fourth straight game, it would require yet another fourth-quarter comeback.

That's what they did. The winning drive began with another boost from Ted Ginn, who returned a punt 40 yards to the Detroit 35. The 49ers already were in Akers' striking distance, but they trailed by four points with a little more than five minutes remaining. Roman called five straight runs with most of them featuring Boone and Sopoaga—approximately 650 pounds between them—as extra blockers. That chipped away at the clock and got the 49ers inside Detroit's 10-yard line. That's where the drive stalled. Gore was cut down for a three-yard loss, Smith threw a short completion to Michael Crabtree, and then came an incompletion on an attempt to receiver Kyle Williams. Now it was fourth down from Detroit's 6-yard line with 1:56 remaining.

Roman called a play on which Smith had two targets aligned to his right. Walker, who had caught the opening touchdown a week earlier against Tampa Bay, was the underneath receiver. His job was to take one step forward and then run a slant to the goal line. The play ended up foreshadowing another throw Smith would make at the goal line to another 49ers tight end. "We liked the big body coming in there," Roman said. "We felt like [Walker] could catch it and muscle his way into the end zone. And Alex just nailed it. He put the ball exactly where it needed to be, so Delanie didn't have to break his stride at all. There was no hesitation. He looked like a real confident guy doing that."

The touchdown was reviewed, but replays showed the ball just clearing the goal line—Lions safety Louis Delmas wrapped around Walker's waist, desperately trying to keep him out of the end zone—before the tight end's right knee touched the turf. After the Lions only were able to muster a four-and-out series on their next possession, Akers hit another field goal with 1:06 remaining to put the 49ers ahead 25–19. A few plays after that, the 49ers had snapped the Lions' winning streak at nine games.

Now it was time for the San Francisco sideline to celebrate. Harbaugh had introduced plenty of themes and slogans to the 49ers that summer. One of them involved passing out light blue, collared work shirts, the kind a mechanic, an electrician, or a machinist might wear. There was even a little oval patch on the right-hand breast with the player's name in red, cursive letters. That was what Harbaugh wanted: a team full of blue-collar workers who enjoyed toil, who didn't mind getting their hands dirty, and who appreciated an honest day's work. Harbaugh explained his philosophy to the players: a workman goes to his job every morning and uses his hands. He busts his ass during his shift and then goes home at day's end with a sense of accomplishment. What do you do when you get home? You grab a cold beer from the fridge and you find your favorite easy chair. But what do you do before you sit down? You untuck your shirt and get comfortable.

He underscored that last part: when the work day is over, you untuck your shirt. It was the 49ers' way of marking the end of the day and a job well done. It became their post-win battle cry. So after the clock ran out in Detroit, players sprinted from the sideline, untucking their shirts as they ran. Boone, the 49ers' extra offensive lineman that year, did exactly that and yelled to Harbaugh, "Untuck your shirt!"

So the head coach followed suit, untucking his shirt, showing a glimpse of his belly in the process, and then enthusiastically chest-bumped the offensive lineman. Harbaugh was the team's head coach, but he often acted like the oldest brother in *The Outsiders*. He was the head of the family for sure, but he also was someone more than willing to throw a few punches during a rumble in the local park. As he belly-bumped his players, Harbaugh was in his element, celebrating with his boys after work had finished for the day. The problem is that Schwartz appeared for the customary postgame handshake between coaches just after Harbaugh's encounter with Boone, when Harbaugh was fully fired up. Harbaugh grabbed Schwartz's right hand and, with an enthusiasm unknown to mankind, gave him a thwack on the back with his left hand. According to Schwartz, he also gave a shout of triumph as they parted, something akin to "Fuck, yeah!"

"I went to congratulate Coach Harbaugh and got shoved out of the way," Schwartz said. "And then I didn't expect an obscenity at that point. So it was a surprise to me at the end of the game."

Schwartz seemed to register what happened for a moment and then raced down the field—a full 40 yards—to angrily confront Harbaugh. Bob Lange, the 49ers' spokesman at the time, was on the field because NFL Films had requested to be in the 49ers' locker room for Harbaugh's postgame speech. Lange said he was trying to make his way to Harbaugh to see if the film crew would be permitted in the visiting locker room and to give the head coach the postgame talking points. "I'm trying to intercept Harbaugh as he was heading into the tunnel," Lange said. "Out of my peripheral vision, I was able to see a white blur: Schwartz. So when I saw the white blur, I just got between them. It was me and Anthony Davis and our security guy, Lou Pezzola."

Schwartz screamed at Harbaugh at the mouth of the stadium tunnel, and players from both teams squared off as if there was going to be a rumble. Linebacker NaVorro Bowman even put his helmet back on and buckled the chinstrap just in case. But enough coaches and security officials got in between the groups to defuse the situation, and eventually the teams went to their respective locker rooms. Harbaugh looked like he wasn't quite sure what had happened and trotted in for his postgame press conference. "Yeah, yeah, I was just really revved up," he explained "It's totally on me. I shook his hand too hard. I really went in, and it was a strong, kind of a slap-grab handshake, kind of like the same as I've been doing with a few of the other [49ers] guys. That was on me, little too hard of a handshake there."

Most players didn't know what had happened at the time. But when they watched the video afterward—the majority of them when they boarded the team plane to San Jose—they smiled at the sight. "At that point it was like, 'That's our coach. That's just who he is,'" Snyder said. "I don't want to say that I loved it, but we rallied around it. It was exciting that our coach was that passionate about what we were doing and how well we were playing."

Said Justin Smith: "He was a different guy. It wasn't businesslike at all. At that point we were just going out and getting after people and we were having fun doing it. And he had our backs, kept it loose, and kept it fun. And I think that was the secret sauce to that year."

Another Harbaugh-ism: he never flew first class. Harbaugh wanted to be known as a regular Joe, a working stiff. So he preferred to fly in coach with the rest of the blue-collar workers. He did that when flying commercially. And he and his staff did that on the 49ers' chartered flights as well. On the way back to the Bay Area, the veteran players got to fly in the front of the plane. Harbaugh, Roman, Vic Fangio, and the coaches were in the coach section. Gore got out of his seat in first class and came back to talk to the coaches. He had run for 141 yards against the Lions, which would be his highest total of the season. "We schemed the shit out of Ndamukong Suh and that defense," Roman said. "And Frank came back and talked to us. And he was saying, 'Man, now I can see where this offense can go.'"

After the Lions game, the 49ers beat the Cleveland Browns and Washington Redskins and then topped a 6–2 New York Giants team at Candlestick Park. When they blew out the Arizona Cardinals 23–7 on November 20, their winning streak had reached eight games, San Francisco's longest since 1997. The 49ers were back.

That streak, however, would end there. The following week, the 49ers were scheduled to play on Thanksgiving night against the Baltimore Ravens. The game would pit Harbaugh against his older brother, John, whose team was 7–3 at the time. It was the first time head-coaching brothers ever faced one another. It was a colossal NFL story. Their parents were interviewed ad nauseum. A pregame handshake was covered like it was the opening ceremony of the Olympics. Reporters called it Harbaughgeddon.

Jim Harbaugh and the 49ers weren't amused. The game was in Baltimore, which meant the 49ers had a short week to prepare and a nearly 3,000-mile trip to make. It was the first time a team had traveled three time zones for a Thanksgiving game since the Los Angeles Rams had gone to Detroit in 1975. "It was very considerate of the NFL to reunite brothers on Thanksgiving," Jim Harbaugh said before the trip. "It's going to be very difficult for our team. No question we drew the short end of the straw on this one. There's just not a lot of time to even think about the warm and fuzzy reunions or the nostalgia of it all."

The 49ers had a walk-through practice in Santa Clara, California, before flying to the East Coast Wednesday. When they landed they took a bus to Johns Hopkins University and had a night practice. "We had to bring out lights so we could practice at night," Joe Staley said. "Then we left. That was all we were able to do that week."

A few days earlier, the 49ers' offense had run 87 plays—about a third more than a typical contest—against the Cardinals. "And we weren't running draws and screens," Roman said. "They were stacking the box. [The Cardinals] had a physical defense, and it was a bloodbath. Then we had to cross the country in three days' time and play a really good defense. We just had no juice. We had nothing. Guys were trying, but we were a tired team at that point."

Smith was sacked nine times by the Ravens ferocious defense, and the 49ers mustered only 170 yards, the lowest output of the season. Still, it looked as if they would hang tight with the home team when Smith connected with Ginn for a 75-yard touchdown that would have given the 49ers a 10–3 lead. The play, however, was called back on a controversial chop-block penalty against Gore, who officials said blocked a Ravens player while guard Chilo Rachal was engaged in his own block of the player. Replays suggested that wasn't the case, and the 49ers never found the end zone that evening. They fell 16–6 but quickly recovered.

They beat the St. Louis Rams at home the following week to clinch a spot in the playoffs and then won three of their next four games, including a *Monday Night Football* victory against the Pittsburgh Steelers, a game that was remarkable for Aldon Smith's two-and-a-half sacks and seven quarterback hits on Ben Roethlisberger and for two power outages—before and during the second quarter—at Candlestick Park that led to 35 minutes in delays. "That cemented it: we are a contender," Snyder said of the 20–3 win against Pittsburgh in Week 15. "We're built for this, we practice harder than anybody in the league, we meet more than anybody in the league. There's a reason for the team's success. And then you throw in the bonding, all that stuff that we created in the off-season, that game sticks out as, 'Okay. We're here. The Niners are back. We beat Pittsburgh in primetime. We're ready for anything. Let's go!'"

In the season finale, which was played on New Year's Day, 2012, the 49ers traveled to St. Louis and won 34–27. The victory turned out to be critical. It meant that the 49ers had barely nudged the New Orleans Saints to be the NFC's No. 2 playoff seed. Both teams finished 13–3, but because of the 49ers' better record in conference play, the Saints had the No. 3 seed and had to play in the wild-card round.

The 49ers not only would get a first-round bye, but they also would host the Saints—the Gregg Williams-led defense that had throttled them in the preseason—if the squads happened to meet in the postseason. And that's exactly what happened.

CHAPTER 5
THE TONY MONTANA SQUAD

In 2020 the hip-hop star Future's net worth was estimated at around $40 million. He's considered one of the genre's most influential artists and has collaborated with everyone from Drake to D.J. Khaled to Beyonce. He won Best Rap Performance at the 2019 Grammy Awards. He fills 20,000-seat arenas. But back in 2011, the rapper, who was born Nayvadius DeMun Wilburn, didn't have much of a following outside of his native Atlanta. He performed in small clubs and bars there and throughout the Southeast and recorded tracks on independent or self-produced albums. Some of the songs were played in the Atlanta strip club Magic City, which has been a launching point for burgeoning rappers from that city.

One of those tunes, titled "Tony Montana," made it into the San Francisco 49ers locker room during the 2011 season. The song is based on *Scarface*, the 1983 film starring Al Pacino as a Cuban refugee-turned-drug kingpin named Tony Montana. Future, who was 28 years old at the time, has described the song's message as "making sure you come out on top some kind of way—even if you have to give everything."

Outside linebacker Ahmad Brooks gets credit for bringing the song to Santa Clara, California. He listened to it constantly at his locker as a way to pump himself up before practices and games. He listened to it so much, in fact, it became a running joke in the locker room. "Ahmad—he's a great guy, but he was kind of in his own world sometimes," said linebacker Blake Costanzo, the ringleader of the 49ers' special teams that year. "And he would blast this song all the time. And we could hear it coming out of his headphones. And it became, 'Dude, Ahmad listens to this song every single day.' And they sing the same words—'Tony Montana, Tony Montana'—over and over. And it just became a little joke to bust on him. It was like, 'Why are you listening to this same silly song every day?'"

Costanzo took the joke a step further when the regular season began. Before a home game, he asked a team official for a favor. He said his birthday was coming up and he'd love it if they played his favorite song, "Tony Montana," at Candlestick Park during the game. That was a fib. Costanzo's birthday was in April. And "Tony Montana" certainly wasn't his favorite song. He just wanted Brooks to hear it come over the stadium sound system. It was meant as a good-natured jab at his fellow linebacker.

That prank worked to perfection. The song came on before a kickoff, and as Costanzo predicted, everyone on special teams started cracking up. It was hilarious. "It was the first kickoff of the game, and we're all just like, 'No way! I can't believe they played it!'" Costanzo said. "And we all started messing around, dancing, whatever. But on that kickoff, Delanie Walker went down and caused a fumble."

The board operator in Candlestick Park noticed the bounce the song had provided the 49ers and he played it again on the team's second kickoff. And then on the third. By the end of the game, it wasn't a gag anymore. It had caught fire. Suddenly, the obscure song didn't belong to Brooks. It had been commandeered by the 49ers special teamers. They began playing it during practices and before kickoffs at the following home game. It became their anthem and they began to refer to themselves as the "Tony Montana Squad." "They started playing it, and we just kind of ran with it," Costanzo said.

The 49ers special teams coordinator at the time was the professorial Brad Seely. His units, however, were anything but conventional. They abounded with swagger and big personalities. There was linebacker Tavares Gooden, who went by TGood and who was known for wearing sunglasses indoors. There was backup running back Anthony Dixon, who preferred to go by his nickname from childhood, Booby. There was backup defensive back C.J. Spillman, who was perhaps the most athletic member of the unit and would finish first among 49ers special teamers that year with 19 tackles. There was Walker, who would go on to become one of the top tight ends in the NFL, but who was also a core special teamer when the season began. And there was Costanzo, the New Jersey native and charismatic leader of the group. He had been in the league four years, playing for the Buffalo Bills and Cleveland Browns before signing with the 49ers in free agency in 2011. Costanzo ended that season as the team's top special teams player, leading the 49ers in solo tackles (10) and knockdowns (27).

The 49ers may have been led by Justin Smith, Patrick Willis, and their defense that season, but the special teams became San Francisco's starter motor, the unit that bounced and swayed and pumped its arms and got the crowd in a lather before games. The Tony Montana Squad literally would kick off the 49ers' victories. They got the parties started. "It became probably the coolest thing I've been a part of in a stadium before," Costanzo said. "I played a lot of special teams during my career. And inside the stadium, people usually go to the bathroom, whatever. But Candlestick—and I heard this from everybody—was the loudest and craziest before kickoffs, which was cool because normally people don't even watch the kickoffs. I remember at one point sitting in the sauna with Patrick Willis…And he's like, 'Man, the kickoff thing is the coolest, hypest thing ever. I'm going to ask Seely if I can get on kickoff coverage.' Patrick Willis even wanted to be on special teams!"

Team officials recognized this as they began preparing to host the New Orleans Saints in the divisional round of the playoffs. They wanted Candlestick Park pulsating like never before during its first postseason game in nine years. As the showdown approached, they hatched a plan to have Future on hand for the game. Paraag Marathe, the team's chief operating officer at the time, sought assent from head coach Jim Harbaugh before finalizing the plan and got advice from one player. Otherwise, it was meant to be a surprise. When the 49ers players spilled onto the field before the opening kickoff, Future would be standing above them on the Candlestick dugout, microphone in hand, singing the song they had used to fire themselves up all season. They cut a check for $35,000—in 2020 booking Future for a gig might cost 20 times that—and figured it would be money well spent if the rapper could help get Candlestick Park even a decibel louder than usual.

There was only one hurdle. The Saints–49ers game was slated to be the first of four contests of the NFL's divisional playoff weekend. It was going to kick off at 1:35 PM. on Saturday. Future already had a gig in Tampa Bay, Florida, at a bar called Club Diamonds that wouldn't end until early the same morning. "We got some good advice," Marathe said. "I don't remember who gave it, but the advice was, 'You should send someone to make sure he gets on that plane.'"

Marathe essentially needed someone to fly to Tampa on Friday night, attend Future's show, befriend the rapper, and make sure he boarded a plane to San Francisco that left at 6:00 AM Eastern Standard Time on the morning of the game. He settled on an employee named Mike Libby, the low man in Marathe's analytics department. At the time, Libby mainly was a salary cap analyst, someone who would research player contracts or come up with statistical ways to predict a college player's success in the NFL. He essentially was a 27-year-old numbers guy, though Marathe had used him on several interesting side projects throughout the years.

One of them came in 2009 when the 49ers were having a hard time signing their first-round draft pick, wide receiver Michael Crabtree. Most rookies ink their initial contracts before training camp begins in late July. Crabtree, however, thought he was worth a lot more than what the 10th overall selection was slotted to earn. He refused to sign his contract, and his holdout lasted throughout the summer and spilled into the regular season. At one point the receiver's agent informed Marathe, the team's contract negotiator, that Crabtree had gone back home to Dallas and was now intent on sitting out the entire 2009 season and re-entering the draft the following year. In other words, he no longer wanted to be on the 49ers roster. So if the team still wanted to sign him, the offer had to be extremely tempting.

Marathe wanted to know whether that was a bluff. So he assigned Libby to perform a stakeout on the absent receiver. He did and he discovered that Crabtree not only remained in the Bay Area, but he also was actively watching the 49ers' games. He obviously still wanted to be part of the team, and Marathe knew he still had the upper hand in negotiations. He also knew he had a dependable foot soldier to send to Tampa to retrieve Future and his entourage. "[Libby] had proven his mettle," Marathe said. "We knew he was the right guy for the job."

"I'm pretty sure it was Paraag that came up with the idea," Libby said. "Paraag comes up with all kinds of crazy ideas. This is one of his crazier ones. But I was sitting in my office on Thursday afternoon, and Paraag walked in and floated this idea to me. And I think he'd already asked some other employees about it. And they're like, 'Hell, no, I'm not going to do this.' And I'm like, 'Yeah, sure. That sounds good.' Basically, they explained it that they were flying in Future to perform at the game. He has a show in Tampa, and it starts at 1:00 AM. They needed me to make sure he got on the plane."

Libby received the go-ahead for the plan on Friday, packed a small overnight bag, and headed for the airport. He arrived at Club Diamonds, which billed itself as an upscale martini bar, after midnight on the day of the game before Future had begun his set. One of his assignments was to make the rapper feel special. He found Future getting ready for his show in a white van parked behind the club and presented him with a Vernon Davis jersey that had been signed by the 49ers tight end. "I gave it to him," Libby said. "And he kind of looked at it with this confused look like, 'Who are you? And why are you giving me this?'"

Future, after all, was from Atlanta and was a Falcons fan. The rapper eventually played his set list, including "Tony Montana," in front of a packed house—about 200 or so patrons. The hip-hop artist and everyone

Following his show, Future gets ready to perform at Candlestick Park—but not before making a 49ers staffer sweat out his arrival. (Mike Libby)

on stage were wearing sweatshirts that said "Astronaut Status," the name of the mixtape he had released just two days earlier. The show ended an hour later. Since the flight wouldn't leave for another four hours, Future and his entourage, including his manager and bodyguard, went to a nearby hotel. The scene was one you'd expect from a young rap star at the beginning of his ascent: partying, girls running around, and a bit of chaos—as well as thick, acrid smoke in the air.

Eventually, Future retired to his room. And then didn't emerge. At around 4:35 AM, Libby climbed inside the limousine that was waiting outside the hotel to take them to the airport for the 6:00 AM flight. He started nervously checking his watch. Future's agent, Orlando, walked out at 5:00 AM, but the star of the show was missing. "I'm like, 'All right, we probably should start getting to the airport, right?'" Libby said. "And Future's nowhere to be found. I'm talking to the manager, and he's like, 'Yeah, he's in his room. It's locked. We can't get in there.' And so it

101

became, 'Oh shit, what are we gonna do? Are we gonna actually miss our flight?' I came out here to do this thing. And now we can't get him out of his room. I wasn't gonna go bang down his door, you know?"

The rapper eventually emerged from the hotel at 5:25 AM wearing the same "Astronaut Status" outfit he had been wearing for the show. He had no bag or cell phone, just a pair of sunglasses. He strolled to the limousine without a care in the world. At that point, it became a cartoon-ish race to the airport. When they arrived no one in Future's group had their boarding passes, which caused another delay. It was now 5:45 AM. The group still hadn't gone through security. It didn't even have boarding passes. Libby was in full flop-sweat mode. "Future," he said. "Do you still want to fly to San Francisco if we miss this flight?"

"We're not gonna miss it, Mike," the rapper replied in a relaxed voice.

He was right. Despite never quickening his stride, Future and the rest of the group walked onto the plane just before the door closed. "It was not fun for me, but Future—he was just this super nice, laid-back, easygoing guy," Libby said. "He was just kind of in his own world, walking slowly, no worries and no stress. Whereas I'm kind of like, 'Oh, shit, I gotta get this guy on the plane!'"

The flight arrived in the Bay Area, and the group got a police escort to the stadium. And when the 49ers emerged from the dugout, there was Future—dressed in the signed Davis jersey that had been presented to him hours earlier—perched above them. The players went crazy when they realized who he was. And already crackling with noise and energy, Candlestick Park rose another two levels in voltage. "Everybody was pumped up," tackle Joe Staley said of the atmosphere. "And I remember going out there for the warm-ups, and the energy in that stadium was unbelievable. There were so many people on the sidelines. It was packed. It was a whole different level from regular-season football. I started getting a little nervous."

"I almost couldn't breathe," said guard Adam Snyder, "just in trying to take in the moment. The fans were insane."

The 49ers won the coin toss and, of course, elected to kick off so that the Tony Montana Squad, swaying back and forth and pulsing with energy as Future sang their anthem, could take the field first. The ball kicked off, and the 49ers' most riveting game of the 21st century was underway. The Saints, who had ranked third in the NFL during the 2011 season in yards per kickoff return, started their average drive on their own 22-yard line in that game and fumbled twice on returns. Costanzo recovered one of the fumbles and forced the other. "I've never been a part of anything that was as amped as it was that day," Costanzo said. "Every possession, every play—it was truly special."

The Future gambit was such a hit the 49ers brought him back the following week for their game against the New York Giants. Libby even got recognition from Harbaugh, who bumped into him in the cafe at the team's headquarters. "Jim had gotten word of the story and he came up to me and said, 'You're the guy that got Future out here,'" Libby said. "And so I went and told him the story. He was wide-eyed the whole time. You know how Jim Harbaugh is. He totally loved it."

Costanzo said he and his teammates never got to meet Future. By the time they got back into the locker room and changed out of their uniforms, he was gone. He may have even been asleep. "What was crazy is that toward the end of the game he was literally tired of singing the song because we scored I don't know how many times," Costanzo said. "So by the end of the game, I think he was only really dancing up there. He wasn't even singing the words at that point."

CHAPTER 6
THE SAINTS COME MARCHING IN

During the 2011 regular season, Gregg Williams' New Orleans Saints defense was as aggressive as it signaled it would be when they thrashed the San Francisco 49ers in an August preseason game. But the Saints offense turned out to be the true bully. It ran up 62 points in a Week Seven rout of the Indianapolis Colts and scored at least 40 points in six other contests. Quarterback Drew Brees surpassed Dan Marino's single-season passing yards mark, running back Darren Sproles set an NFL record in all-purpose yards, and the Saints offense as a whole broke the record for yards from scrimmage in a single season.

Tight end Jimmy Graham, fast, tall, and an excellent leaper, dueled with Rob Gronkowski that year for most receiving yards ever by a tight end with Gronkowski narrowly edging out Graham 1,327 yards to 1,310. (Those marks later would be surpassed by 49ers tight end George Kittle, who had 1,377 yards in 2018.) The 2011 Saints widely were considered the best team in the franchise's history, and two years after the team's first Super Bowl title, the city of New Orleans was anticipating another. The Saints stomped the Detroit Lions 45–28 in the wild-card round of the playoffs. If they took care of the 49ers, there was a good possibility they'd host the NFC Championship Game at the Superdome, where they felt they were invincible. And that season they were. The Saints didn't lose a single game at home. Their average margin of victory there was 23 points. "That was the best offense we had in New Orleans—ever," offensive lineman Zach Strief said. "I don't think there was ever any question. And then even more than that, as good as the numbers were that year, it was really the last eight games where that started happening. We were 5–3 going into Week Eight, including a loss at one point to a Rams team that hadn't won a game yet. It was really non-NFL like. We were scoring so many points so easily in those games. What made it really special was how good it was leading into the playoffs. It was an accelerating team with all kinds of momentum going into the playoffs. I think that's what made it unique. We were playing our best football, and the football we were playing was historically good."

The 49ers agreed. Heading into that playoff game, defensive coordinator Vic Fangio, who had been an NFL defensive assistant since 1986, said New Orleans' offense was the best he had ever prepared to play. Even though the 49ers were the home team and had been awarded a first-round bye, they were the underdogs. The Saints were favored by 3 ½ points. "There was no bones about Vic," 49ers offensive coordinator Greg Roman said. "He'd say, 'Hey, get ready to score some points.' They were that good. They were a machine."

Of course, Fangio's defense also was the best one he had ever coached. The secondary that had been thrown together a week into training camp quickly coalesced and played as if they had been teammates for a decade. The 49ers tied for the league lead with 38 takeaways that season, and cornerback Carlos Rogers, criticized mercilessly in Washington for his futility at coming up with interceptions while playing for the Redskins, had six during the 2011 season, tying Dashon Goldson for the team lead.

Outside linebacker Aldon Smith finished his rookie season with the team lead in sacks while playing next to veteran Justin Smith, who finished with 7.5 sacks of his own. Perhaps most significantly, offenses simply couldn't run the ball against Fangio's unit, which had two of the best and fastest inside linebackers in the league in Patrick Willis and NaVorro Bowman. Opponents averaged a league-low 77.3 yards a game on the ground against San Francisco in 2011, had trouble picking up first downs, and truly struggled to find the end zone. The first time an opposing tailback ran for a touchdown that season was in the fourth quarter of Week 16 when Marshawn Lynch of the Seattle Seahawks plunged in from four yards out.

Heading into the divisional playoff game, the storyline was so obvious it could be seen from space: it was the Saints' high-flying offense that had averaged 34.2 points a game against a fast and ferocious 49ers defense that had given up an average of 14.3 points a contest. The 49ers defenders realized they had to take a page from Williams' playbook: they had to rough up their opponent. "If we were going to beat the New Orleans Saints, we knew that we had to be physical with those guys," safety Donte Whitner said. "That was the only chance that we had—if we were physical. And Vic Fangio preached that to us. The night before the game, specifically, he said, 'If we allow this team to take the football and go out and score on the first drive, we will lose this football game.'"

Willis described the defense's mind-set to reporters. "Every time we step on that field, it's about not giving the other teams anything," he said. "It's something that Coach Harbaugh talks about all of the time—cruelty. It's not giving another person what they want."

The game, however, began as Fangio feared. Sproles gained five yards on the Saints' first snap. Drew Brees completed a 10-yard pass on the second. Chris Ivory ran for another four yards on the third. Brees and the offense chipped away at San Francisco's defense for five yards here, four yards there, and in 11 plays, the Saints already were in the shadow of the 49ers' end zone. On third down on the 49ers' 7-yard line, Brees hit running back Pierre Thomas in stride in the flat. He reached the 2-yard line, and it seemed as if his momentum would take him into the endzone and give the Saints not just an early lead, but also a declaration that even the 49ers' vaunted defense was no match for their offensive juggernaut.

Instead, Thomas was met by Whitner just short of the goal line. Whitner was the smaller man. In fact, he was the smallest man on the field at that time. He was shorter by two inches than even Brees, who is famously undersized for a quarterback. But he was thick, tough, and already had a reputation as a vicious hitter. He won the collision. The impact drove Thomas backward two yards, and like a boxer stung by a wicked right cross to his chin, the running back crumpled limply to the ground as if in slow motion and lost the ball in the process. Willis recovered the fumble at the 2-yard line, and the outcome the 49ers had dreaded the most—a quick Saints score to start the game—had been averted.

The 49ers defense had flexed its muscles. Whitner literally did so as he strutted off the field following the takeaway. "I remember seeing [defensive backs coach] Ed Donatell on the sideline," he said. "And Ed Donatell said, 'That just won the football game for us.' He actually said that to me after that play."

The rest of the game was full of similarly memorable, momentous plays. The most iconic moment in the careers of Alex Smith, Justin Smith, Joe Staley, and Graham occurred in this contest. Whitner's came first. The tackle on Thomas was his finest, most famous play, the one that will forever flash in the minds of 49ers fans whenever his name is mentioned. The blow not only sent the wobbly Thomas out of the game for good, but it also ended up staggering the Saints—who had been rolling at the start—for a full quarter. New Orleans ran the ball four times on the opening drive but only 10 times after that. "It was the end of our running game," Strief said. "It made moving the football very difficult. We were one-dimensional. All we talked about all week was how important balance was going to be. And then—*boom*—just like that, not only did we lose our first scoring drive, but we lost the running game. And it made things really difficult. Ultimately, it put us in a tough position offensively. And that's why we threw the ball 63 times. That was pretty far from the gameplan going in."

Staley described his emotions going in. "I just remember being really nervous in the beginning of the game, like, 'I hope this goes well,'" he said. "I just didn't know what to expect. Then that big hit happened, and the nerves calmed down, and it was like we were back in football."

Said Fangio of Whitner's hit: "It had the tangible effect of taking three points off the board, number one. And number two, any time you can make a hit of that magnitude at any point in the game, but especially early, it sends a message."

That message? "Now you know you're in for a long day," Whitner said. "That's what we wanted. Whenever you have a big hit, whether you're on the offensive side of the ball or a defender, it does something to you…It does something to your psyche, especially receivers and quarterbacks and skill position guys. That's what we wanted. Any time we played New Orleans, we knew they were more of a finesse football team. If you go back to some of our games that we played in the Superdome, we always had to be extremely physical with those guys if we wanted to win those games."

As Thomas lay dazed in the fetal position on the Candlestick turf, Whitner showed his muscles and preened for the 49ers' sideline. The crowd went berserk, and the 49ers defense seemed to puff up, too. "That kind of limited a lot of guys, their mind-set, the rest of the game," Goldson said. "Not only the coordinator and his play calling, but guys didn't want to come across the middle. They didn't want to come across me and Donte back there."

On the next Saints' series, Aldon Smith sacked Brees on third down to force a three-and-out sequence. On the drive after that, Goldson stepped in front of a deep throw from Brees and returned the interception to the New Orleans 4-yard line. The takeaway broke down another psychological barrier because it ended Brees' NFL-record streak of 226 postseason passes without an interception, a streak that had begun five years earlier. In the second quarter, Whitner delivered another monstrous hit on another Saints runner, Sproles, causing a fumble that was later reversed on replay review.

Later in the game, Justin Smith produced perhaps the most memorable play of his career. Entering the contest Smith had been one of the few 49ers who had ever been to the playoffs, having done so in a losing effort when he was a fifth-year player with the Cincinnati Bengals in

2005. During the season first-round draft pick Aldon Smith, who lined up next to Justin Smith, became the 49ers' most feared pass rusher. He was quick and powerful and, despite playing only on passing downs, finished the season with a team-best 14 sacks. Many of them came on plays, in which he would loop inside Justin Smith. The older player was more than willing to help clear a path to the quarterback. "That developed as the year went on, knowing what Aldon could do and knowing there was some stuff that I'd be able to open up for him, basically grabbing guys and this and that," Justin Smith said. "At that point I really didn't care about sacks and stats because I was on the back end of my career. I just wanted to win."

The veteran defender, however, still had a few moves of his own. And of all the players on the field that day against New Orleans, Smith, who was 32 and in his 11th season, knew how fleeting postseason appearances could be. He battled against the Saints as if the game might be his last shot at a title. Inside the defensive line meeting room, Smith's signature move was known as "The Bludgeon." It wasn't fancy. The weight room king, Smith was the strongest player on the team and he got to the quarterback with brute strength. On one particular play, he moved 315-pound Saints left tackle Jermon Bushrod backward as if he were on roller skates, reached past Bushrod to grab the back of Brees' jersey, and pulled both adversaries—more than 500 pounds together—to the ground with one mighty tug. "That was Justin," Adam Snyder said. "If you had to pick one play out of his career, that would be it. If you had to put who he is in an image, that's it. And the thing with Bushrod was he was an excellent player. I mean, he was a Pro Bowl guy. It wasn't an average left tackle. This guy was legit. The thing about Justin's move is it happened to everybody he's played. If you played Justin Smith, that happened to you. It happened to me in practice every single day. He had a couple of moves that he was so good at that there was almost nothing you could do. You just kind of hold on for dear life."

"It was so physical," Strief said of the game. "I remember sitting on the bench and looking at Jahri Evans and going…'When I was a kid going to NFL games, this is what I envisioned it was like.' And I don't know how many games in your life are like that. When you're a kid, it seems so impossibly difficult. It seems so much bigger than reality. And so many games don't necessarily feel like that. That game felt like what I anticipated the NFL would be like. And I still say—despite the result—being in the game with the adrenaline and the intensity, that was my favorite game that I ever played in. I don't think I ever played in a game that I felt more emotionally invested in."

At one point early on, the 49ers thought that Graham, whom they considered the most dangerous Saints weapon, would join Thomas in the locker room with a concussion. Following a long incompletion to Graham along the right sideline with Whitner in coverage, the tight end landed hard on his head and got to his knees slowly before being helped off the field. Whitner figured Graham was finished for the day, too. "I know for a fact that he had a concussion," he said. "And any time we played those guys—and I know it sounds bad—but we would hand out concussions to those guys. We weren't trying to purposely do it. It was just being caught up in the football game. But that's how we played. That's the only way you beat those high-powered offenses. You have to be extremely physical with them. And you have to know it's going to be a long day."

Said Rogers of Graham's condition: "He should have been out of that game. He was wobbly. They should have taken him out of the game."

It would've been a different scenario in 2020. "If that happened today, you'd say, 'Oh, we lost him. They're not going to let him back,'" Strief said. "The reality then was: Jimmy was a tough guy, had played through a lot of injuries in his career. I think we all felt like he was going to come back."

Those defensive plays epitomized what the 49ers did to the Saints to open the game. They throttled the greatest offense the NFL had ever seen. When David Akers kicked a 24-yard field goal a little less than a minute into the second quarter, Staley looked up at the scoreboard to find the 49ers leading 17–0. "I remember thinking on the sideline during the middle quarters, *Well, this is kind of anticlimactic,*" Staley said. "My now-wife—she used to be my girlfriend then—I got her tickets. And their tickets were directly across from me on the other side of the field behind the bench. And they had a big old sign. It said something like "Staley is Foxy" because the game was on FOX. And they were hammered. And I remember being up 17–0, the stadium is going crazy, and I remember looking across the field and seeing Carrie laughing and holding up the sign like, 'Oh this is so easy! This is so much fun!' Then they came back."

Snyder had a similar sentiment. "I remember thinking, *It can't be that easy,*" Snyder said. "I know they're going to come back. Yeah, maybe there was a little bit of confidence that built up in that first quarter, but you can never be too confident when you're playing an opponent like Drew Brees."

Snyder was right. Graham left the game with assistance after his hard fall in the first quarter, but he was back in the second. Like their star tight end, Brees and the New Orleans offense regained their equilibrium and began to march again. Willis, the 49ers' fastest linebacker, had been assigned the task of covering Graham, even practicing his cornerback skills with Donatell and the defensive backs in the lead-up to the game. But as brilliant as the linebacker was, the assignment was next to impossible. Willis stood a little over 6'1". Graham was 6'7" with long arms and a vertical jump of a basketball power forward, which he played at the University of Miami for four seasons.

On the Saints' first touchdown of the game, Brees merely tossed the ball into the middle of the end zone from the 14-yard line, allowing

Graham to sky over Willis for the score. After a 49ers' three-and-out series, the Saints went on a seven-play drive that ended with Brees lofting a perfect pass over the outstretched arm of cornerback Chris Culliver and into the hands of receiver Marques Colston for a 25-yard touchdown. Suddenly, it was 17–14. The Saints had lifted themselves off the canvas, and it was the 49ers who went into halftime on their heels.

One Shot

Jim Harbaugh wasn't exactly hip with current culture. With tan slacks, a black sweatshirt, and a whistle around his neck, he dressed like a coach from the 1950s. His sweatshirt may as well have had "COACH" written in block letters across the chest. His idea of good music—what Harbaugh referred to as "a real toe tapper"—was a Johnny Cash tune. But there was one modern song that he tapped his toes to: Eminem's "Lose Yourself." He liked the message that competitors might only get a momentary chance to shine, and when that opportunity comes, they have to seize it with both hands. Except Harbaugh referred to the song not as "Lose Yourself" but as "One Shot," one of its oft-repeated lyrics. It was a joke among the team that Harbaugh took part in. "Hey, let's play that song, 'One Shot,'" he would say.

"One Shot" also became the theme of halftime during the New Orleans Saints game. Fiery, passionate Knute Rockne-like locker room speeches, in which an individual rises and exhorts a spellbound team, are a staple of football cinema. Unfortunately, they're mostly inaccurate. If there's a good speech, it usually comes after the game as the head coach passes out gameballs in the winning locker room. Halftimes are businesslike with various positions splitting off into groups and going over the Xs and Os of the first half. An NFL halftime lasts only 12 minutes; there's usually no time for fist-pounding and soaring oration.

Halftime of the Saints–49ers game was different and worthy of a sports drama. The driver of it was Vernon Davis, who had scored on a 49-yard touchdown catch in the first quarter and who was crackling with energy as he stepped into the cramped locker room. Davis wheeled around the room and warned everyone not to let the opportunity in front of them—their lead over the Saints—slip away. His refrain was: "one shot," which he wrote on a white board in the middle of the locker room. "That was the message," Davis said after the game. "You only get one shot. If you don't take advantage of it, you go home. There was a lot of fire within me at that moment, and something just hit, and I had to let it out. When you're a leader on this team, that's what you're supposed to do. You're supposed to step up, lead the team in times like that."

The speech, however, couldn't jump-start any real momentum. The 49ers scored a field goal in the third quarter after one special teams ace, Blake Costanzo, knocked the ball loose from Darren Sproles on a punt return, and another, Colin Jones, recovered at New Orleans' 26-yard line. It was the 49ers' fifth—and final—takeaway of the afternoon. Something else happened in the third quarter that didn't get much attention after the game. Receiver Ted Ginn collided with a Saints player late in the third quarter and had to be helped off the field with a knee injury. Ginn had only 19 catches that season, and his absence didn't have much effect on offense. But he also was the 49ers' punt returner, and in that facet of the game his loss would turn out to be monumental. Kyle Williams took over both roles from that point forth.

As the game slipped into the fourth quarter, it had turned into a grudge match. Neither offense could sustain any momentum over a nearly 20-minute span of the contest. They merely managed to trade field goals. After the 49ers hit theirs, a 37 yarder by David Akers, the score was 23–17 in favor of San Francisco with 7:36 remaining.

Following the ensuing kickoff, Drew Brees completed three straight passes to receivers Devery Henderson, Marques Colston, and Robert

Meachem, the longest of which was 13 yards. That wasn't ideal for the 49ers, but it was allowable. Up until that drive, New Orleans' longest play had been Colston's 25-yard touchdown. Otherwise the 49ers defense had kept the Saints playmakers penned in. That was what Vic Fangio's defense was predicated on: you can allow completions, but keep everything in front of you. Most crucial of all was to not allow any big plays—or "explosives" in NFL jargon.

On second down from the San Francisco 44-yard line, one of the Saints' playmakers finally broke out of the 49ers' cage. Sproles caught a short pass from Brees, scampered out of tackle attempts by Dashon Goldson and Donte Whitner, and went into the end zone for New Orleans' longest gain of the day. Suddenly, the Saints were up 24–23 for their first lead of the day. Brees had chipped away for nearly four quarters, and the 49ers defense was starting to collapse. There only was a little more than four minutes remaining. Now it was the Saints, who finally felt in control. "For most of that game, it was really this heavyweight fight," Zach Strief said. "Then all of a sudden, there's all these explosive plays that didn't exist early in the game. And we'd just had Sproles break a tackle and take it all the way. And we thought when *that* happened, that might be the game winner because, to be honest with you, San Francisco's offense wasn't very good, and they hadn't been great in that game."

He was right. The 49ers' identity that season was built around Justin Smith and the defense. The offense's job was to keep things simple, grind out long drives on the ground with Frank Gore, and avoid mistakes. And Alex Smith played that role brilliantly. He threw only five interceptions that season, and the 49ers tied an NFL record by committing only 10 turnovers all year. Smith also hadn't been asked to throw the ball deep down field or to win games with his arm. While Brees had a league-high 46 touchdown passes during the regular season, Smith had only 17, which was the 17th most in the NFL and the fewest of any quarterback who started all 16 games that year. Instead, the 49ers leaned on Akers' leg that season. He kicked an NFL-record 44 field goals in the regular season, meaning he outscored Smith by a wide margin. Throughout his career with the 49ers, Smith had developed a negative reputation as a game manager. Some in the organization derisively referred to him as "Captain Checkdown" because instead of going for the big, aggressive gain he would settle for the smaller, safer one. On the New Orleans sideline, no one thought Smith and the 49ers offense would—or could—respond. The Saints' offense, after all, was a Lamborghini; the 49ers' offense was a Volvo station wagon. If it became a race between the two, one would be left in the dust.

At the same time, the 49ers defense was starting to lose confidence. Goldson and Whitner, the heroes of the opening quarter, had broken the cardinal rule of the defense on Sproles' long catch and run: they'd allowed an offensive player to wriggle free for an explosive-play touchdown. As they walked back to the bench, their shoulders drooped, and their early-game swagger was gone. "I remember getting to the sideline and talking to Whit like, 'Damn, man, I messed up. I missed that tackle,'" Goldson said. "And I remember him saying, 'Man, shit, don't worry about it. We got this.'"

Said Fangio: "I thought we were playing them really well. We held them to 17 points midway through the fourth quarter. And then all hell breaks loose."

If the 49ers were going to win their first playoff game in nine seasons, an offense that had merely been safe and steady all season was going to have to win it. San Francisco had one thing in its favor: Gregg Williams. The Saints defensive coordinator wanted his players frothing at the mouth with aggression. Months afterward, audio was released of Williams' speech to the Saints defenders the day before the game. It seemed to corroborate the allegations made in the Bountygate scandal. In profane and blunt language, Williams issued a veritable hit list of return man Kyle Williams, who had suffered a concussion a few weeks earlier. He said: "We need to find out in the first two series of the game, that little wide receiver, No. 10, about his concussion. We need to fucking put a lick on him right now. He needs to decide. He needs to fucking decide."

That was not Williams' only target:

> **On Gore:** "We've got to do everything in the world to make sure we kill Frank Gore's head. We want him running sideways. We want his head sideways."
>
> **On running back Kendall Hunter:** "Little 32, we're going to knock the fuck out of him. He has no idea what he's in for."
>
> **On receiver Michael Crabtree:** "We need to decide whether Crabtree wants to be a fake-ass prima donna, or he wants to be a tough guy. We need to find out. He becomes human when we fuckin' take out that outside ACL."
>
> **On Davis:** "We need to decide how many times we can bull rush and we can fuckin' put Vernon Davis' ankles over the pile."
>
> Most damning of all, Williams is described as rubbing his thumb against his index finger—implying there is cash to be made—before talking about quarterback Alex Smith. "We hit fuckin' Smith right there," Williams said while allegedly pointing to his chin. "Remember me. I got the first one. I got the first one. Go get it. Go lay that motherfucker out." He returned to Smith later in his speech and referenced the game the teams played in August. "Alex Smith, in the preseason game, when you guys fuckin' avalanched that motherfucker, had eyes that big. You all saw 'em."

Williams was just as aggressive in the playoff game as he was the preseason, sending blitzers at Smith on nearly every play. To the delight of the 49ers—and the astonishment of some of the Saints—the defensive coordinator continued to do so even after New Orleans took the lead. The 49ers took over at their own 20-yard line with 4:02 remaining and two timeouts. On first down Smith hit Hunter on a short pass the running back turned into a 13-yard gain. On the next play Williams called what's known as a zero blitz, meaning there is no deep safety on the play. The extra defenders were blitzing the quarterback, and the defensive backs and linebackers were in man-to-man coverage.

Smith got rid of the ball quickly on a pass to Davis, who had a step on the Saints safety. The pass fell incomplete, and the Saints sideline breathed a sigh of relief. Davis was perhaps the only 49ers offensive player capable of scoring from anywhere on the field, and they had just dodged a bullet. On the next play, however, Williams again dialed a zero blitz. This time Smith didn't miss. He delivered a deep ball down the left side to Davis, who hauled in the pass and was pushed out of bounds along the Saints sideline for a gain of 37 yards. The 49ers were on the New Orleans 30-yard line. In a one-point contest, their stodgy offense was now in field-goal range, and it had only taken three plays to get there. "We called zero blitzes twice in a row!" Strief said. "We called it the first time and we got lucky. Alex overthrows Vernon Davis running across the field. And we came right back behind it and we called it again."

"They were doing some pretty exotic blitz packages that we were having some trouble with ID-ing and figuring out," Joe Staley said. "But when they were doing that, they were in man to man. And that's why Vernon was able to rip off some of those plays."

The 49ers had more surprises in store. After Davis' big gain, the 49ers ran the ball twice to set up a third-and-3 play from New Orleans' 23-yard line. Before the snap the 49ers were penalized five yards for having too many men in the huddle. The 49ers called their second timeout of the half. At the sideline they decided to use the first of two plays they had installed specifically for the Saints game. In that situation—third and 8 from the 28-yard line—the 49ers wanted a play, in which they had a chance of picking up the first down but also one, in which there was no chance of a sack that would take them out of field-goal range. They knew the Saints were prone to blitzing and playing man-to-man coverage, which meant the defensive backs would be trailing the receivers with their backs turned to the quarterback. The 49ers decided to call a quarterback sweep.

There were two concerns. The first was that Gregg Williams and the Saints defense had been overloading one side of the line of scrimmage with a blitzer throughout the game. If the 49ers ran the sweep in the same direction from which the Saints were sending pressure, they'd be running straight into the teeth of the defense. "It would have gotten blown up," Greg Roman said. "I wish I could say it was feel on my part. It was a calculated guess."

The other problem was that since San Francisco had installed the play in the run-up to the game, the coaches thought it would be a surprise. It turned out the Saints knew it—or something like it—was coming. Center Jonathan Goodwin said he talked to Saints defensive end Will Smith the following offseason, and Smith told him the Saints defensive line was ready for a quarterback run in that situation.

It didn't matter. After taking the snap, Alex Smith took off to his left at the same time a Saints defensive back was blitzing from his right. Roman had guessed correctly. As the quarterback moved out of the backfield, Will Smith started running down the line of scrimmage to his right to head him off before the first-down marker. It was receiver Kyle Williams' job to come in from the outside with a crack-back block on any lineman who had a chance at the quarterback. Will Smith was 6'3", 285 pounds; Williams was 5'10", 186. But his block froze the defensive lineman and got Alex Smith started on his journey. "For a receiver, especially a receiver of Kyle's size, to make that block on a guy Will's size, it was huge," Goodwin said.

Said Roman: "We had had some protection issues, and I was definitely expecting one of those overload blitzes. So it was just a roll of the dice. It was really well-executed. Kyle Williams had a great block. Staley obviously led the way."

Williams' block allowed Smith to pick up the first down. But as he reached the marker, the quarterback realized he might have a shot for something bigger. There was only one other Saints defender, a safety, between him and the end zone, and Staley was barreling toward that defender. At one point in his life, Staley had been a high school track star, setting school records in three races, including a 21.9-second time in the 200 meters. He began his career at Central Michigan as a tight end before being moved to tackle prior to his sophomore season, which is to say he didn't move like a lumbering 300-pound lineman. "He was running like a gazelle," Roman said. "And as the crowd got louder and louder, it seemed like he ran faster and faster."

The play developed better than anyone could have hoped. "I thought it was going to be pretty open. I thought we were going to get a first down," Staley said. "And once I got around the corner, there was no one there, and I was like, 'Shit, we're going to get a touchdown.' Then it was a matter of finding the closest dude."

Said Goodwin: "I remember just looking up and seeing Alex running with Joe. And as soon as Joe made the cut, I think I threw my arms up because I knew after that it was a touchdown. Not many tackles in the NFL are going to make that block that far downfield on a safety."

"I was on the backside of the play," Adam Snyder said. "My responsibility is to hit the d-lineman, leave him to the tackle, and get up to the second level. I was trailing behind everybody because they had gotten out in front, so I was a couple of yards behind everybody. To see it from that perspective was insane because it was wide open. We all knew what was going to happen next."

After Alex Smith rushed for a touchdown against the New Orleans Saints, Greg Roman said Candlestick Park "went ballistic." (Kym Fortino / San Francisco 49ers)

Staley cut down the safety at the sideline, allowing Smith to sprint unscathed into the end zone for what at that point was the longest run of his career. "As we ran down the sideline, I just remember thinking, 'Get the first, get the first, get the first,'" Alex Smith said. "I was prepared to do whatever it took— jump, dive, whatever—just to get a first down. And then you look up, and there's nobody there. It was such a strange feeling."

"I saw the safety coming down, and he was the only one there," Staley said. "And I made the block. And I remember, I made the block, rolled, and—there's a picture of it—and I'm on my back looking up, and Alex is right there, and he's got a fucking grin. And my face is like, 'Holy shit!' I get goose bumps thinking about it."

Said Roman: "I was up in the booth, but Candlestick Park went insane. As Alex Smith ran from the 30 to the 20, you could see everybody getting up. And the place just went ballistic—like I'd never seen it, well, until the touchdown later."

Staley thought it would be the defining moment of his career. It seemed like it would be Smith's too. They hugged and celebrated in the end zone as the stadium exploded with electricity and noise. It was a riveting, spectacular way to end a game. Only it was far from over.

The 49ers failed at a two-point conversion that would have put them up by seven points. They now led 29–24 with 2:07 left. When New Orleans got the ball back, Brees connected with Sproles and Colston for first downs. Then from the Saints' 34-yard line, he reared back and threw deep down the middle of the field to Jimmy Graham, who was being trailed by Patrick Willis.

As the ball arrived, both Willis and Whitner, who was converging from deep in the 49ers' defensive backfield, leaped to swat the ball away but missed. They took themselves out of the play, and the ball instead was plucked out of the air by the Saints tight end, who now had no defenders—at least none who were still on their feet—near him. He took off and wasn't touched as he went into the end zone for a 66-yard score. "Playing against an offense like that, you know you're not going to hold them down forever," Whitner said. "It was always creeping into the back of your mind that if we don't continue to do what we're supposed to do then we can probably lose this football game. And when they threw that football to Jimmy Graham, and he scored, now we're thinking like, *Uh oh. Here we go. We didn't hold them down. We didn't do our part to finish that football game."*

Graham punctuated the touchdown by slamming the ball so hard over the crossbar the whole structure began swaying back and forth. Candlestick Park, which seconds earlier had been as loud and raucous as it had ever been, suddenly was so silent that for the next 60 seconds you could hear the groans and squeaks of the ancient goal posts as they continued to shiver from Graham's celebration. It was as if an earthquake had struck the north end zone. Even the Saints were stunned. "It was disbelief, like, 'I can't believe this just happened.'" Strief said. "Knowing the defense that we played and the difficulty getting behind that defense… really the only thing that couldn't happen for San Fran was that exact play: this long, down-the-middle, over-everyone's-head type deal because we weren't really moving the ball super efficiently against that front."

Longtime New Orleans sportswriter Jeff Duncan thought the Graham touchdown was one for the ages. "I just remember thinking, *this is going to be one of the greatest plays in the history of the organization,*" Duncan said. "When it occurred, the way it occurred, the comeback—it seemed like it was going to be the exclamation point on maybe the greatest Saints win in the franchise's history, certainly in the playoffs."

The 49ers offensive players had been upbeat and assured when they had taken the field on the previous drive. There had been more than four minutes to play at that point, and they felt they could move the ball for a score. As they walked onto the field following Graham's 66-yard score, the swagger had evaporated into the January evening. There was only 1:32 remaining, and following a two-point conversion from Brees to Sproles, the 49ers trailed 32–29. They started their final drive from their own 15-yard line. "On the [Smith] touchdown drive, everyone was confident that we'd go down there and score a touchdown," Staley said. "But after that happened, everyone was like, 'Ohhhhhhh, shit.' This is the way my brain thinks, which isn't healthy…It's not a way to play football, I don't think. But it works for me. The whole time, all I'm thinking is: *Don't be the fucking reason you lose this game.* So I'm super, super focused on doing whatever I can to not get a penalty, not give up a sack, not be the reason things go bad."

Said Snyder: "A little bit of panic sets in. You lean on your teammates at that point. You lean on the guy that's leading the huddle. And for most of my career, that was Alex Smith. I couldn't think of a better guy to lean on because he's never wavered. It happened multiple times over my career where he's said, 'Here we go, boys. Let's go.' He had that look on his face. To have someone that even-keeled with that level of confidence leading the huddle, it starts to settle down that panic a little bit."

Despite the difficult situation the 49ers found themselves in, there was still time on the clock. "I definitely remember being on the sideline thinking, *You've gotta be kidding me*," Alex Smith said, "because we all felt like the drive before was the game winner. And to have it flipped on us so fast was just like, it couldn't be true. But I do remember with where we got the football thinking, *there's enough time here to get a couple completions, and we can take a shot at the end zone.* At that point I was still thinking more of a Hail Mary."

The first two plays didn't convert any of Smith's detractors. He checked down to Gore for a short gain on first down and then did the same on second down. The two completions gained 18 yards, but they also burned 42 seconds, and the 49ers were on their 33-yard line and nowhere near where they needed to be to attempt a game-tying field goal. The 49ers offense had been designed to be plodding because it usually had a lead late in a contest and wanted to burn the clock. Now it had to go fast. "If you go back and watch that drive, San Francisco didn't even look like it had a two-minute [offense] installed in that game," Strief said. "I mean, they throw the ball all over the middle. There's an incomplete pass. It's a bunch of really unproductive stuff in that moment at a time they needed to go down and score. And you feel that, 'Man, we got 'em. This is not what they're made to do.' And it wasn't. It wasn't an offense that was built to explosively move down the field. You watch the first two plays, and it was almost funny. I mean, they're not even trying to get down the field."

Gregg Williams, however, kept creating opportunities for his opponent. On second down he blitzed again, leaving Davis in yet another one-on-one situation with Malcolm Jenkins, the Saints safety. Jenkins was a former first-round pick, one of the top safeties in the league, and a leader on the New Orleans defense, but he couldn't cover Davis one on one. No safety could. Davis had a run a 4.38-second 40-yard dash prior to the 2006 draft, which would have been considered a smoldering time for a feathery, 177-pound wideout. Davis was a chiseled, 250 pounds and he knew how to throw his weight around. "That was a route they call a high cross," Davis said. "It was meant for man to man. Malcolm Jenkins was covering me during that time. I pushed up on him and got some good separation."

Smith hit the tight end in stride. Davis outran Jenkins, then cut up the Saints sideline before being forced out of bounds at New Orleans' 20-yard line. People who were standing along the sideline said they felt a breeze kick up as Davis blew past. There were 31 seconds left, and the 49ers had new life. "They had been in prevent [defense]," Smith said. "And you're kind of thinking, *My god, it's gonna be tough sledding with the clock just against us, and maybe we'll get a chance to get the Hail Mary off.* And I remember we lined up, and I just couldn't believe that they were playing man [coverage] and just being so thankful that they were playing man again."

Roman had the same thought. "I was like, 'Wow, they're in man,'" Roman said. "And Alex just nailed him on the deep cross. That was a huge chunk. That got us into field-goal range."

"I remember thinking, *I can't believe he's blitzing us!*" Goodwin said. "Of course, [Gregg Williams] doesn't know this, but in practices it used to seem like when we were in two-minute drives we would get a lot of checkdowns. So Alex making that throw kind of caught me off guard. But I guess it was partly because we were getting blitzed."

Strief was watching from the Saints sideline as Davis streaked by. "It's a really good example of: live by the sword, die by the sword," Strief said. "It's maybe the most devastating play that I was a part of because it just didn't make any sense in that moment to let that offense move down the field like that, which they hadn't been able to do all day. It was a frustrating deal, and that's what made that game so fun: things kept happening that you never anticipated could happen. And it happened over and over and over again."

Said Snyder: "The funny thing about playing offensive line is that you don't see when that happens because we're so busy making sure our guy's not killing the quarterback. So the roar of the crowd is always what gets my attention, jolts me a little bit. My thing was to sprint as hard as I could to get to the ball, and I just remember being so happy for Vernon and my excitement for him. I was probably jumping around and giving him high-fives. That lasted a couple of seconds. Then reality sets in, and it's like, there's more to do. We've got to score."

On first down Smith threw a short pass to Gore that brought the 49ers to the 14-yard line. On second down he spiked the ball to stop the clock with 14 seconds remaining. The 49ers had an opportunity for an easy field goal that would have sent the game to overtime. Instead, they decided to go for the kill shot. "We were like, 'We've got to win this now,'" Roman said. "That was the mantra: we need to win this thing now."

The quarterbacks coach at the time, Geep Chryst, had spent the previous five years as the tight ends coach for the Carolina Panthers, who play in the same division as the Saints. Chryst was familiar with their defensive tendencies and knew that—as aggressive as Gregg Williams was—he liked to play a bit more conservatively in the red zone. The 49ers guessed that the Saints would only rush three or four defensive linemen. And they figured they'd plant one of their safeties, Roman Harper, the same one who had drilled Smith in the center of his back to begin the preseason opener, on the goal line. At that stage in the game, the Saints were only interested in one thing: keeping the 49ers out of the end zone and forcing them to try a short field goal that would send the game to overtime.

So Roman called the second play that had been installed especially for the Saints game. Most teams that have the play in their arsenal use it to throw to the outside receiver. The 49ers, however, wanted the ball to go to Davis, the player who lined up in the slot. "It was a play specifically meant for their two-deep coverage in the red zone," Roman said. "The key was that it was a bang-bang play. It was going to be the tightest of tight windows, and that was going to be all Alex Smith and Vernon Davis. And Alex—he just let it rip."

Smith dropped back three steps, planted his right foot, and let go of the ball just as Davis made his cut toward the center of the end zone. The ball zipped so closely past one of the shallow defenders, linebacker Scott Shanle, that Shanle later would say he felt it whistle past his head. Davis, the ball, and Harper all arrived at the same point simultaneously, and Harper was blasted backward. While he remained on the ground in the end zone for several seconds, Davis popped up with the ball cradled in his right hand. He had hung on. Ninety minutes after his emotional "one shot" shot speech in the locker room, he had done exactly what he had preached: he had seized the moment and come up with the 49ers' greatest play of the 21st century.

His catch immediately triggered memories of the one Terrell Owens had made with four seconds remaining in a 1998 wild-card playoff against the Green Bay Packers in the same end zone at Candlestick Park, one in which the receiver was crunched as the ball arrived but somehow held on for the score. Like Owens that day, Davis rose from the hit in tears and didn't stop crying for the next 30 minutes. "I just kept telling myself, 'one shot,'" Davis said after the game. "'The team is depending on you. Vernon, the team is calling your name. You have to step up and make the play. You have to take charge.'…It was big. Everyone was counting on me."

His catch was dubbed the Vernon Post. "Utter jubilation," Roman said, "first year, hadn't been in the playoffs in forever, against this juggernaut who had blown us out in the first preseason game, tried to rub our nose in it, and it was pretty special for everybody."

Even before the game, players had noted how packed the sidelines were and how animated the crowd was. It was the 49ers' first playoff game in nine years and with every big play—Whitner's hit, Justin Smith's takedown, Alex Smith's touchdown run—the noise level ratcheted upward another level. When Davis crashed into the end zone, the volume became deafening, and the venerable stadium, which had seen so many tremendous victories and so many remarkable catches, rattled in celebration. "It definitely was the loudest point," Goodwin said. "And it was the first time all game that I definitely felt like we were going to win the game. I remember breaking off of the celebration in the end zone and yelling…I don't know what I yelled. I was just ecstatic."

For Staley it was a blur. "I didn't see anything," Staley said. "All I remember is hearing the crowd go absolutely insane. I thought the crowd was loud when Alex scored. I thought there was crazy energy then. But I've never heard anything like that. It was absolutely nuts."

Whitner will never forget Davis' reaction. "I just remember Vernon still crying like a little baby. He was crying all through the locker room. It was like that catch T.O. had. It was a rendition of that. He was crying and crying and crying."

Even Alex Smith, usually so composed and so straight-laced, was overcome with emotion. After congratulating Davis, he ran up to Saints safeties who had tormented him in the preseason opener and allowed himself a rare moment of trash talk. After all, there were only nine seconds left. "There was a lot of smack talk going on in the game, and I'm definitely not one to be talking," Smith said. "But that was such an emotional roller coaster there at the end, and I'd definitely taken some shots. So to hit that touchdown, you obviously know that's the last nail in the coffin. And it just started coming out of me."

Still, the game already had so many unbelievable twists and turns that Goodwin wanted to make sure there wasn't another. The ex-Saints lineman hunted down special teams coordinator Brad Seely on the sideline and warned him that the Saints had a trick play kickoff return designed for instances exactly like the one they were in. "It was basically their version of the Music City Miracle," Goodwin said. "And I was telling Coach Seely about it, that if Colston was on the field, it would be a throw back. And sure enough, he was on the field."

It didn't matter. Akers squibbed the kickoff, and coverage specialist C.J. Spillman crushed Robert Meachem, ending the game and sending the 49ers to the NFC Championship Game for the first time since 1997.

Like many who were on the field that day, Strief called it the best game he had ever been a part of. It certainly was the most emotionally draining. "That season those were the two best teams in football," he said. "And I think one of us knocked the other out, and the other one destroyed the team that won before they played their next game. It was an absolute dogfight. It was hands down the most physical game I ever played in."

Inside Candlestick Park's absurdly cramped visiting locker room, the Saints players moved like zombies. Some of them sat stunned on stools and were still in their jerseys and shoulder pads 30 minutes after the game had ended. Eye black had streaked down some of their faces. It was hard to tell if the tracks were made by sweat or tears. "That was the only time in my career that I had to apologize to a reporter after a game because I really jumped on Jen Hale, who's a sideline reporter for FOX now," Strief said. "She asked me a question, and I was sitting at my locker and I was just not ready to deal with it yet and I kind of snapped a little bit. And I had to call her later in the week and apologize. There were so many big, big emotions that happened one right after the other. That's why that game is memorable."

The mood was different across the hallway. There was the elation and revelry you'd expect when a team topples a mighty opponent and does so to win its first playoff game in nine years. But the emotion wasn't uniform. Tears continued to pour from Davis, who had to compose himself before walking into the postgame press conference, where he told reporters his famous catch ought to be known as "The Grab."

The defensive players, meanwhile, reacted like they had cheated death. After holding the Saints to 17 points through three-and-a-half quarters, they had given up 15 in the final four minutes. Nothing like that had happened to them all season.

Whitner, whose first-quarter hit will go down as one of the 10 greatest plays in franchise history, and Goldson, who had intercepted Brees and finished with a game-high 11 tackles, should have celebrated their team's triumphs. Instead Whitner was left trying to pump up Goldson as if they were complicit in some terrible crime. "Everyone was all hyped up," Goldson said. "And I just remember sitting in front of our lockers and talking to Donte like, 'Man, we escaped one, bro. We almost cost [us] that game.' And he's like, 'I know, but we did it.' Everybody was excited and jumping around, and I was just sitting in my chair like, 'Man, that could have been bad, that one play.'"

Goodwin had the final word to the Saints. As the season wore on and as he bonded with Staley, Snyder, Alex Smith, and the rest of the 49ers offensive linemen, the sensation he had felt in early August—that he was making a terrible mistake by leaving New Orleans—began to fade away. He not only realized he was in the right spot, but also as the regular season drew to a close, he knew it was his destiny to help defeat his former team. "Once we secured the bye, it was pretty obvious to me that we would end up playing them in the first round," Goodwin said. "I struggle to put it into words. But it was a very emotional game for me, an emotional two weeks. I knew we were going to play them."

In the second quarter, however, Goodwin came up limping, following a short pass to Gore. He had pulled a calf muscle and needed help from the team's trainers getting to the sideline. Snyder stepped in at center, and Chilo Rachal filled in at right guard. The injury would have knocked Goodwin out of the game for good against any other opponent. This, however, was special. This was fate. "The worst thing that could happen would have been to watch the team that you decided to leave go to the Super Bowl," Goodwin said. "So I had to stop them from doing that."

When the third quarter commenced, Goodwin was back in the center of the offensive line and he finished out the game. Afterward, he was one of the last players to leave the locker room. The entrance to the 49ers locker room in Candlestick Park, which has since been torn down, was across a narrow, cluttered hallway from the entrance to the visitors' locker room. As he exited, Goodwin bumped into Mickey Loomis, the Saints general manager who didn't want to pay Goodwin what the center felt he was worth and whom Goodwin initially blamed for his departure from his beloved New Orleans. Six months later the animosity was gone. Goodwin had found a new home. His conversation with Loomis was brief and pleasant. "He told me he knew there was no way in the world I wasn't coming back into the game," Goodwin recalled with a laugh. "He said he missed having me in New Orleans and he said there was no way I was going to stay out of that game."

CHAPTER 7
A GIANT PUNCH IN THE GUT

A s the San Francisco 49ers began preparing for their next opponent, the New York Giants, they felt as if they'd been kissed by destiny. They had been the ultimate underdogs entering the season. They'd been a six-win team in 2010, a team with a new coaching staff, one that was maligned by the lockout as much as any other, one that had had its nose shoved in the dirt by the New Orleans Saints in its very first outing. Now the 49ers were one win away from the Super Bowl and feeling as powerful as they ever had.

After all, they'd lost only three games. The first defeat—in Week Two to the Dallas Cowboys—was explained away by the fact that they were new at that point and hadn't yet coalesced. The Thanksgiving night loss to the Baltimore Ravens was sloughed off as unfair scheduling: having to fly across the country for a Thursday game. The final loss—at the Arizona Cardinals in Week 14—was simply a lapse in concentration and some oddball plays.

The 49ers, for example, called a brilliant fake field goal in the second quarter that saw holder Andy Lee throw a pass to a wide open Jonathan Goodwin, one of the linemen on the play. The veteran center rumbled in for an apparent touchdown, the first of his long career. Big-guy touchdowns are the four-leaf clovers of NFL football. They're rare, and Goodwin was mobbed by deliriously happy teammates. But the officials blew the play dead midway through because Arizona had challenged the previous completion from Alex Smith to Kyle Williams, and the mechanism for halting the game for a replay had malfunctioned. The field-goal attempt had to be repeated, the 49ers couldn't possibly attempt another fake, and David Akers' 50-yard attempt sailed wide right, his first miss from 50 or more yards that season. On the very next play, the Cardinals struck with a 60-yard touchdown pass. It was their first score in a game they would go on to win by two points.

That rotten-fortune sequence, however, was very much an exception for the 49ers in 2011. Not only were they a good team, they also were a lucky one. Only one Week One starter—receiver Josh Morgan—suffered a major injury, a broken bone in his leg in a Week Five win against the Tampa Bay Buccaneers, during the year. Otherwise, they were a remarkably healthy group with Jim Harbaugh on several occasions stepping to the postgame lectern and announcing the team had "dodged a bullet" with what could have been a significant injury.

They also were opportunistic on the field. Justin Smith poked the ball from Philadelphia Eagles receiver Jeremy Maclin when the 49ers needed exactly that type of miracle play late in the game in Philadelphia in Week Four. When they needed a big stop at the end of a Week 10 game against the Giants, Smith raised his arm and batted away a fourth-down pass from Eli Manning deep in San Francisco territory in the closing seconds. With the Seahawks driving at the end of a Christmas Eve game in Seattle and the 49ers clinging to a two-point lead, linebacker Larry Grant sacked quarterback Tarvaris Jackson and caused a fumble that preserved the win. Then in the first round of the playoffs, Donte Whitner, Alex Smith, Vernon Davis, and a host of other players delivered critical plays when the 49ers absolutely needed them. "The attitude had changed," defensive lineman Justin Smith said of the 2011 season. "It went from, 'Oh, shit, something bad is gonna happen in the game' to 'We're gonna win it no matter what.' And that kind of just happened over the course of the year and got us rolling."

It was as if the team had its own guardian angel that season. So in the run-up to the Giants game, the 49ers began to feel as if a trip to the Super Bowl was preordained. "We found out we were playing the Giants after the Saints game," tackle Joe Staley said. "And we felt like the Saints were the team to beat. And after we beat them, we knew we would be playing at home and we felt confident, maybe a bit too confident."

The game against the Giants began like the Saints game ended. On the 49ers' second drive, Alex Smith dropped back, quickly looked to his left, and then floated a perfect pass down the right sideline to Davis, who somehow managed to stay in bounds—his heal hovered above the white boundary marker, but his toe never touched the line—and dash into the end zone for a 73-yard score.

The tight end leaped over the line of photographers behind the end zone, then hopped on top of a camera stand, and crossed his arms in a proud pose. The gesture drew a penalty flag, but no one cared. Davis, Alex Smith, and the 49ers were still on fire. Nothing had cooled off since the New Orleans game. "I remember thinking after that play,'" Staley said, "*We're still rolling.*"

After the touchdown to Davis, however, the 49ers' luck finally began to wobble. On their next drive, they tried a trick play—an end-around, in which tailback Kendall Hunter tossed the ball to Williams, who was moving in the opposite direction. Williams flubbed the pitch but some-how managed to snatch the ball from defensive lineman Osi Umenyiora, who was in position to pounce on it at the San Francisco 24-yard line. The sequence was a harbinger of what was to come. "That was brutal," offensive coordinator Greg Roman said. "[Williams] lined up too tight on that play, and it was too quick of a pitch. But that could have been the difference in the game."

Early in the second quarter, the Giants tied the game with a short pass to tight end Bear Pascoe, a one-time 49ers draft pick, and then took their first lead on a 31-yard field goal just before halftime. The 49ers regained the advantage early in the third quarter on another big throw from Smith to Davis. This one was from 28 yards out, and the tight end clutched the ball to his chest just before being hit by a Giants safety in the end zone.

After that it was the defense's chance to make a big play. The 49ers had forced an NFL-high 38 takeaways in the regular season and had taken the ball from the Saints five times in the first playoff game. With a minute to play in the third quarter of the NFC Championship Game, the defensive line flushed Manning from the pocket on third down. He

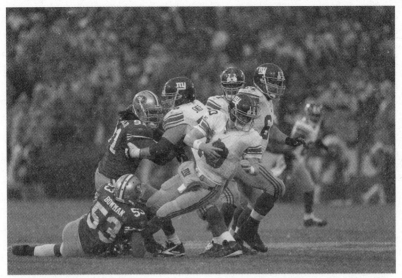

The 49ers defense records one of their six sacks against Eli Manning in the NFC Championship Game. (Terrell Lloyd / San Francisco 49ers)

threw a poor pass into the middle of the field that seemed like an easy interception for Tarell Brown, the cornerback on the play. The problem was that it was just as tempting for safety Dashon Goldson, who was converging from center field. They arrived at the same time, and Goldson, the larger man, flattened Brown, who lay on the ground for nearly five minutes before eventually being helped to his feet. Goldson gently cradled his teammate's head as he was being led off the field and then apologized to him on the bench between series.

Brown didn't return, and his absence proved costly. The 49ers defense, which seemed to grow stronger as the game wore on and the rain fell harder, forced a three-and-out series when the Giants got the ball back. At that point the game was well into the fourth quarter, and all of New York's possessions since halftime had ended in punts. In fact, the Giants' best drive of the half had lasted five plays and gained 22 yards.

Still, all of the breaks began going New York's way as a gray day turned to night, and the sheets of mist coming off the San Francisco Bay became a little more intense. It started with a Steve Weatherford punt, which began bouncing well short of the 49ers' return man, Williams. He had been conspicuously audacious in fielding the ball a week earlier against the Saints when he entered the game for the injured Ted Ginn. There were no ramifications in that contest, but it served as foreshadowing for this one.

Williams was overly aggressive on Weatherford's fourth-quarter punt, allowing himself to get too close to the bouncing ball. He halted at the last second as the ball hopped toward him, but the Giants scooped it up while claiming it had struck the returner. Replay reviews showed they were right. The ball barely, perhaps imperceptibly for Williams, glanced off his right knee at San Francisco's 29-yard line. Williams was incredulous and insisted—even after watching the replay on the Candlestick Park video board—that the ball hadn't struck him. "Are you kidding me?" He screamed to referee Ed Hochuli.

The Giants had gotten no farther than their own 32-yard line to that point in the second half. Now they were already within striking distance of a field goal. Six plays later they did better than that when Manning dropped back, had time to throw, and connected with receiver Mario Manningham on a post route in the middle of the end zone. Manningham beat cornerback Tramaine Brock, who had come into the contest after Brown had been knocked out by his own teammate, for the score. Brock had never started a game before, and the Giants took advantage. Now they were up 17–14 with 8:34 to play.

Williams had committed a colossal mistake, but he tried to make up for it on the ensuing kickoff. He fielded the ball at the 5-yard-line, then found a seam up the left hash marks, and didn't go down until he reached San Francisco's 45. Alex Smith took that momentum and gained 17 yards on a quarterback scramble on first down. On the next play, Hunter swung around to his left, picked up big blocks by tight ends Davis and Delanie Walker, and gained 18 yards. His and Smith's gain were the 49ers' longest runs of the contest. The drive, however, bogged down in the red zone. Smith tried to hit receiver Michael Crabtree on the right side on third down, but Crabtree was driven out of bounds well short of the first-down marker. The 49ers had to settle for an Akers field goal that tied the game at 17.

The completion to Crabtree, which occurred with six minutes remaining, was the 49ers' first to a wide receiver in the game. It also marked the ninth time they had failed to convert a third down. They wouldn't convert any in regulation time that day, and afterward Crabtree, who finished with a lowly three receiving yards, grumbled that the quarterback was at fault. Smith, he said, needed to be more aggressive. "Sometimes you've just got to move the ball," Crabtree told reporters. "You've got to make plays. You've got to give people chances to make plays."

New York's defense, however, was nothing like the one the 49ers had faced a week earlier. Whereas the Saints blitzed constantly—and many would argue recklessly—and in doing so gave the 49ers opportunities for big counterpunches, the Giants had perhaps the best defensive line in football and could generate pressure with just four rushers. The other seven defenders could drop back into coverage and take away the 49ers' passing lanes. In the wild-card game that year, the Giants had held the Atlanta Falcons to two points. They had traveled to Green Bay the following week and knocked off the Packers, one of the Super Bowl favorites, in freezing temperatures. New York's defensive line seemed custom-built for bad-weather games in January and they were proving that again at dreary, drizzly Candlestick Park. "The Giants defense was very simple and very good," Roman said. "Their defensive front was outstanding."

Early in the fourth quarter, the 49ers sent both Justin Smith and nose tackle Isaac Sopoaga onto the field on offense so they could help pick up a first down on third and 1. Smith was one of the strongest players in the league at that point in his career. Sopoaga, who weighed 330 pounds, was the 49ers' biggest defensive player. When they lined up on offense, it gave the 49ers the ultimate heavy jumbo package, one designed to intimidate. The 49ers wanted to show they were the tougher of the two bullies on the field that day. The Smith-Sopoaga package was an uppercut that would send a message. But as Smith fired off the line of scrimmage, he easily was tossed aside by the Giants' Mathias Kiwanuka, and New York stuffed tailback Anthony Dixon for no gain. The Saints defense had been wild and undisciplined. The Giants were calm and stout. It was as if the 49ers were playing a version of themselves. "Linval Joseph, Justin Tuck, Osi Umenyiora—they were big, athletic," lineman Adam Snyder said. "Justin Tuck was kind of like Aaron Donald before Aaron Donald—not an oversized defensive tackle, just a guy who was super athletic and quick with his hands. It reminded me of Aldon, just a guy who was good with his hands and quick with his feet and strong. It was one of those games where you just had to do everything right. We had to execute every single play. We had to play the perfect game to beat them. When you get to the postseason, there's something about a team that starts to build. And they build and they build and they build…and then they explode. That was the Giants that year."

Manning, however, didn't have any more success than Alex Smith and the 49ers offense. As the final minutes of the fourth quarter began ticking down, all he could orchestrate were futile three-and-out series. When the Giants got the ball back yet again with 3:04 remaining and the score still 17–17, he was sacked by Patrick Willis for 11 yards. On second and long, he threw a ball in the flat to tailback Ahmad Bradshaw.

Defensive coordinator Vic Fangio's defense was built on taking advantage of exactly that type of play. His linebackers and safeties were swift and excellent at swarming ball carriers, and they did so against Bradshaw. Goldson and Brock zipped forward to stop the running back, and linebacker NaVorro Bowman arrived to finish him off. The linebacker did more than that. He reached his right arm into Bradshaw's chest and pried the ball loose at the Giants' 20-yard line like a man starting a lawnmower.

It was the type of momentous play the 49ers, especially the defense, had consistently delivered throughout the season. It was the playoff version of Justin Smith's forced fumble in Philadelphia. The 49ers hadn't had a takeaway up to that point against the Giants, but this one was massive. Mark Hittner, the head linesman, thought it was a fumble. He was the closest official to the play and immediately came running toward the pile and threw a blue handkerchief, thereby marking the spot of the turnover. There was a little more than two minutes remaining. If the 49ers had taken over at that spot, they at least would have forced the Giants to burn their two remaining timeouts and would have attempted a short, go-ahead field goal. Akers had the finest season of his career that year, set the all-time record for field goals made with 44, and was voted to the Pro Bowl. Bowman's strip effectively would have sent the 49ers to the Super Bowl.

It didn't happen. Another official rushed into the scrum and ruled that the play had been blown dead because Bradshaw's forward momentum had stopped. Hochuli, the referee, sided with the second official, and the Giants never lost possession. To this day it's one of the plays that haunts Bowman. "I just always thought the refs were out to get me," Bowman would say later while noting he was at the center of an equally questionable call in the NFC Championship Game in Seattle two years later.

The 49ers had two more chances in regulation; the Giants had one more. But the respective defenses had grown too powerful, and neither quarterback could move the ball or even fire off a pass. Manning was sacked six times and knocked to the ground on another six plays. By the end of the fourth quarter, his left shoulder pad had been stained a dingy gray from being driven into the Candlestick muck so many times. At one point he rose from a hit and desperately called a timeout. It was like something out of a football comedy. His helmet had rotated a quarter turn around his face, and his chinstrap was wrapped around his nose as he tried to find the nearest official. That's how discombobulated the 49ers defense had made him. "Number one, hats off to Eli," said Justin Smith, who had a sack and four quarterback hits in the game. "I mean, we beat the hell out of him. And we were trying to beat the hell out of him and get after him, and he just kept getting up. He's done that several times in the playoffs. And I'm like, 'That throw's got to be coming out of his ass.' I mean, how in the hell do you get these passes down the sideline like this when we're draped all over him?"

"It's one of those boxing matches where you watch all 15 rounds," Snyder said. "And it's just slug after slug after slug. It's nothing exciting. No knockdowns. No knockouts. But it's just two heavyweight contenders just unloading on each other. It's kind of boring. But it's methodical."

The same thing happened in overtime. When Smith sacked Manning for a 10-yard loss on the Giants' second possession, he leaned back, raised both fists toward the heavens, and unleashed a yell that could be heard above the crowd noise. Smith was like a creature out of Greek mythology: the more it rained, the more tense the game became, the stronger and more powerful he grew.

His sack prompted the Giants to punt for the 12th—and final time—of the game. Kyle Williams fielded it cleanly. But after three steps, New York's Jacquian Williams stuck his right arm toward the 49ers return man's belly and knocked the ball free. Kyle Williams lunged back to retrieve it, but it was too late. The Giants already had swarmed on top of the loose ball at the San Francisco 24-yard line. There was no big hit on the play or on Williams' previous muff. But after the game, the Giants made it clear that they were targeting Williams, who at 5'10", 186 pounds was the 49ers' lightest player and who had a history of concussions. "The thing is: we knew he had four concussions. So that was our biggest thing: to take him out of the game," Jacquian Williams said.

The 49ers, a team that had led the league in takeaways during the season and had given the ball away an NFL-record-low 10 times, found themselves on the wrong side of the turnover ratio at the end of their biggest game of the year. They had coughed up two fumbles to the Giants and had no takeaways in return. New York capitalized off of Williams' first muff with a touchdown. On the second they needed only a field goal to win the game in overtime. Five plays after the fumble, Lawrence Tynes knocked in his attempt from 31 yards, and Candlestick Park, so rowdy and raucous a week earlier, fell silent.

The magical season suddenly was over.

When the final whistle blew, the players and coaches walked off the sideline to shake hands with their Giants counterparts and to offer quiet, good luck wishes for the upcoming Super Bowl. Kyle Williams, however, took off for the sideline at a full sprint. As he approached the tunnel that leads to the locker room, catcalls and boos rained down from the stands. It was a sign of things to come. Players had begun using Twitter four years earlier. It initially was viewed as a wonderful way to communicate directly with fans. No longer did athletes need the media to be an intermediary to relay thoughts and news. Players could control the message themselves and could communicate directly with their backers. But the two-way street also had an ugly and sinister side. Fans and followers could reach out to the players. Most offered encouragement to Williams, but many others went immediately to his timeline with vicious—and menacing—comments.

> @KyleWilliams_10. I hope you, youre wife, kids and family die,
> you deserve it

@KyleWilliams_10 two costly fumbles #reallydude? Enjoy the entire offseason knowing YOU cost us the Super Bowl I pray we resign Ginn #smh

Jim Harbaugh, please give @KyleWilliams_10 the game ball. And make sure it explodes when he gets in his car.

Williams didn't hear any of the hatred as he came off the Candlestick Park field. He was running too fast. He sped down the tunnel, through the locker room, and into the small, cramped training room in the back. He sat on one of the tables in a daze. A few minutes later, the rest of the players started filing in. Williams could hear the curses and shouts of disgust first filling up the narrow tunnel to the locker room and then the locker room itself. He heard tight end Delanie Walker ask where Williams was. Walker's voice wasn't threatening. No, this was the closest, most tight-knit team the 49ers had fielded since their glory years. And not even a gaffe—or two—that cost them a trip to the Super Bowl was going to rip them apart.

The first person who walked into the training room to find Williams was the defensive line coach, Jim Tomsula, whom the 49ers would surprisingly tap to be their head coach two years later. The avuncular Tomsula had taken a difficult, winding path to become an NFL coach. He had once lived out of his car and sold carpets as a side job to support his family. He was self-effacing, approachable, and quick with a story or wisecrack. He was a favorite of the players.

He didn't sugarcoat things with Williams or offer empty platitudes. Tomsula told him the sting would be severe, but that what he had just experienced in the end was merely a game. There were more important things to worry about. As Tomsula wrapped up his talk, players began entering the small room. First came Willis, then Alex Smith, and then Bowman and Walker. Soon, there was a line of players filing into the tiny space to put a hand on Williams' shoulder and to whisper a word of encouragement. "It's easy to pin those types of things on kickers or punt returners because it's such a highlighted play," Snyder said. "It's easy to pin it on him and say, 'You blew it!' Well, no. I embraced him. I gave him a big hug and said, 'Hey, listen, dude. One or two plays don't win or lose a game. We had chances.' You try to talk him out of whatever mood he's in. It was a tough place to be in, and I know he felt responsible."

About 10 minutes later, the doors of the locker room opened up, and the media—local, national, and the throng that had arrived from New York—entered. Williams was still in a daze. But he stood at his locker and faced the phalanx of cameras that encircled him. "I use Kyle Williams to this day as an example to players about being a stand-up human being even in the toughest time of his life," the team's public relations director, Bob Lange, said. "When you take ownership for your mistakes like he did, it humanizes you. It allows people to forgive you a little more quickly. I mean, what are people going to say when you say, 'I screwed up?'"

After the game Williams' teammates noted how many other mistakes contributed to the loss. Years later the players haven't changed their stance. "As a football player, you realize that good plays and bad plays happen," Staley said. "I felt really bad for him because I know how fans are, especially with a big loss like that. Obviously, you expect everything to go right all the time. Sometimes the ball just bounces wrong."

Said Alex Smith, one of the first to file into the training room to try to comfort Williams: "I mean, it was just weird, nasty Candlestick weather, and the poor kid muffs some, and he was trying to be a play-maker. And he had contributed so much up to that point. So I think everybody felt for him and comforted him, and not only did it happen after the game, but even the next day when everyone was cleaning out their lockers."

Still, Williams' fumble and Tynes' overtime kick snuffed out the magic of the 2011 season. The players on that squad say it was the most fun, most unique, most connected team they'd been a part of, and there was a firm sense that the season would end—could only end—with a Super Bowl win. The loss to the Giants was like suddenly waking from an exhilarating dream. Players like Blake Costanzo and Snyder would become free agents and would not be back the following season. "It speaks to the character of the men we had in the locker and to the coaches that created that—whatever the 'that' was that year, the special-ness, the bond," Snyder said. "Those types of teams, I feel like, only happen once in a while. And it was the greatest team I've ever been a part of, the greatest season I've ever been a part of. Those types of things don't come around very often. It was a perfect storm of everything going right, which is why I thought, *this is our year. This is it.*"

CHAPTER 8
A STAR IS BORN

"He's going to be famous someday." Ada Klatt said those words shortly before her death in 1988. She had been in poor health, had suffered a series of strokes, and had become non-conversant, almost child-like in her final days at age 84. But her words that cold, Wisconsin winter day seemed to come from someone—or even somewhere—else, and they struck like a thunderclap. They were spoken matter of factly in a strong voice. It was as if the temperature in the room suddenly dropped, and a chill raced down the spine of her granddaughter, Teresa Kaepernick.

Teresa and her husband, Rick, had recently adopted a months-old boy after the couple had lost two infant boys to heart disease. Their new son named Colin was born on November 3, 1987 in Milwaukee. Just four months later, Teresa brought the baby on a visit to her grandmother in New London, Wisconsin. Teresa sat him down in the middle of a room. The women were amazed the child already could sit on his own. That's when Klatt, who had been cooing and giggling along with the infant, abruptly changed her demeanor and made her prophecy. "It was the way she said it," Teresa said. "She said it like she knew it. I guess that's what was so memorable about it. I never forgot she said it and I repeated it over the years to my family members. And as it turns out, she knew what she was talking about."

It became part of the family lore, and the event would be rehashed during phone calls and at family gatherings as Colin excelled at Pitman High School in Turlock, California; set records at the University of Nevada; and became San Francisco 49ers coach Jim Harbaugh's hand-picked quarterback in the 2011 draft.

Kaepernick's rookie season was quiet. The combination of the lock-out and a leg injury the quarterback had suffered at Nevada limited his exposure. He attempted only five passes in 2011—all of them in mop-up duty at the end of blowout wins. The 2012 season would be different. After all, the 49ers hadn't drafted him early in the second round to have him hold a clipboard on the sideline. Offensive coordinator Greg Roman wanted another weapon on offense—a quarterback who was dangerous on the hoof—and he began sending Kaepernick into games.

At first it was for a snap or two. Against the Green Bay Packers in the season opener, he carried the ball once for 17 yards, a tiny nibble compared to the massive bites he would take out of the Packers later that season. Three weeks later, Kaepernick had five carries for 50 yards in a win against the New York Jets, and No. 7 scored his first NFL touchdown on a seven-yard run in the second quarter.

A year earlier, the 49ers offense had been bland and basic. Apart from the dramatic playoff win against the New Orleans Saints, its assignment was to avoid mistakes and let the defense win the games. The offense was to be seen and not heard. The formula changed in 2012. The offense started to become just as powerful as the defense. In Week Five against the Buffalo Bills, the 49ers rolled up more yards (621) in one game than any team in franchise history. No offense designed by Bill Walsh or run by Joe Montana had ever been as prolific in a single game. The 49ers also became the first NFL team that day to finish with at least 300 passing yards and 300 rushing yards in the same contest. Kaepernick scored a touchdown—this time on a 16-yard run—in that game, too.

But at that point in the season, he was merely a gadget player, someone Roman would send in when he felt the offense needed a jolt. The 49ers remained Alex Smith's squad. He had won over teammates at Camp Alex a year earlier, had electrified fans by outdueling the Saints' Drew Brees in the playoffs, and in 2012 was off to his best season in the NFL.

Still, there were reasons to believe the 49ers coaches weren't fully sold on Smith as their starter. During the offseason Harbaugh and Roman secretly had traveled to North Carolina to evaluate then-free agent quarterback Peyton Manning, who was coming off a shoulder injury. After he chose to sign with the Denver Broncos, Manning called Harbaugh to inform him of his decision. Harbaugh testily said he and Roman were merely "evaluating" Manning, who would go on to win a Super Bowl in Denver.

Then during the season, *Sports Illustrated* ran a story that said the 49ers coaches still didn't fully trust Smith as their starter and that Smith's confidence was wavering as a result. The quarterback seemed to put that notion to rest in the very next game, a 24–3 win against the Arizona Cardinals, one in which he connected on 18-of-19 pass attempts for 232 yards. His only incompletion was a drop by tight end Delanie Walker. Smith set an NFL record at the time for completion percentage (94.7) for a quarterback with a minimum of 15 attempts. A few days later, he was named the NFC Offensive Player of the Week, the first time in an eight-year career the former No. 1 overall pick ever had won the weekly honor. After the Cardinals game, Harbaugh jumped at the chance to dismiss any doubts about his faith in Smith. "I don't think there ever was a question there," he said. "It was just a lot of gobble, gobble, turkey, just gobble, gobble, gobble turkey. That paints a pretty good picture. He's a very confident guy."

Harbaugh continued to playfully pound away on the quarterback's shoulder pads in pregame warm-ups in an effort to psyche him up, a weekly event the television cameras ravenously ate up. The coach also continued to pump him up after games in his remarks to the media. "Eighteen of 19—I have never seen that," Harbaugh gushed after the win against the Cardinals. "I don't know how you play much better. It was a fantastic game by him."

Harbaugh's support, however, was soon to be tested. In a November 11 game against the St. Louis Rams at Candlestick Park, Smith scrambled for four yards on first down at the end of the first quarter. As he began his slide, linebacker Jo-Lonn Dunbar barreled into the back of the quarterback's helmet. Smith was shaken. He grimaced and grabbed at his facemask but remained in the game. He said he felt fine at that point. As the 49ers' drive continued, however, his eyesight began to get fuzzy, and his field of vision started to narrow. He tried to blink through the issue, but it grew progressively worse, including on a quarterback sneak on fourth down, in which he absorbed another blow to the head. He ended up playing five more snaps. The last came when he found Michael Crabtree in the end zone for a 14-yard touchdown pass. He was operating on instinct at that point and could barely make out the receiver. "I literally was guessing," Smith said. "I couldn't see anybody, I couldn't focus. I felt like there were like 30 defenders. I had this crazy, uncomfortable feeling. And somehow we drive down, and then I throw a touchdown pass. I have no idea how this happened. I mean, it was just pure luck."

When he returned to the bench following the score, he knew his outing was over. He had a concussion. "At this point it had been a chunk of time since the hit, and it's not going away," Smith said. "And I'm kind of freaking out. It's weird to not have your eyes be able to focus in and do what you want."

Kaepernick entered the game with 6:31 to go in the half. He was neither terrific nor terrible. He completed 11-of-17 passes for 117 yards and ran for 66 yards, including a seven-yard touchdown in the fourth quarter. Any enthusiasm about the young quarterback's first significant playing time was muted by the outcome: a 24–24 tie. Afterward, Smith couldn't remember chunks of the game. He suffered headaches throughout the week. He knew he had a lingering concussion, and that playing the following week and exposing himself to more blows to the head would be a bad move. He also knew that sitting out the following game was risky because it would open the door for Kaepernick to take his job.

Smith was no fool. Kaepernick was the younger, cheaper alternative. Harbaugh had become enamored with him in the run-up to the 2011 draft, traveling to Reno, Nevada, for a workout. There the one-time

NFL quarterback and the soon-to-be NFL quarterback had a friendly but spirited competition to see who could throw the most spirals or hit the goal post from various spots on the field. The two hit it off to the point where the 49ers traded up to draft Kaepernick early in the second round in 2011.

Despite Harbaugh's often over-the-top praise of Smith, the veteran quarterback knew that everyone affiliated with him—Mike Nolan, Scot McCloughan, the offensive assistants who were on staff in 2005—had been ousted long ago. Those running the team in 2012 had a stake in only one quarterback, Kaepernick. There was a reason coaches were giving Kaepernick a handful of snaps a game: to prepare him for a time when he would take over the starting role from Smith. "Alex struggled with that," Smith's wife, Elizabeth, recalled of the fateful week. "It was, 'It's like I'd be giving him the job. That's what I'd be doing.' But Alex also is not an idiot and he said, 'Why would I risk the future health of my brain for that?' We had long conversations about it. I said I'd rather you never play again than go risk getting another concussion on top of a concussion, which studies show is the worst possible thing you can do."

So Smith sat out the ensuing Chicago Bears game with a significant amount of trepidation about his job status but also with a bit of faith. After all, hadn't he built up a mountain of goodwill with Harbaugh and the 49ers during the lockout the summer prior? And hadn't he performed heroically in the playoffs? Wasn't he in the midst of the best season of his career? Surely, the team would go back to him the following week against the Saints, the very team he had helped topple in January that year, when he was fully recovered from his concussion. "Harbaugh was looking for a reason to start Kap, and I think this kind of fell into his lap," Joe Staley, a close friend of Smith's, said about the episode. "They basically told him to take the week off, make sure you're really good, and get ready for New Orleans."

There were other reasons to believe it would only be a one-week hiatus for Smith. Kaepernick, after all, was known as a running quarterback. That's what he had done at Nevada, becoming the first quarterback in Division I history with more than 10,000 passing yards and more than 4,000 rushing yards. He also tied former Nebraska quarterback and Heisman Trophy winner Eric Crouch's record for most career rushing touchdowns by a quarterback with 59.

When he did throw, Kaepernick didn't exactly exhibit a delicate touch. He had the most powerful arm in the 2011 NFL Draft—stronger even than that of the No. 1 pick, Auburn's Cam Newton. But he didn't show a lot of nuance in practice. A pass into the flat to a running back was fired at the same velocity as one 55 yards down the field. The fastballs practically left a vapor trail. Receivers had to worry about broken fingers when Kaepernick was targeting them.

With that in mind, expectations were modest for his first NFL start, which would come at home against the Bears on *Monday Night Football.* Former 49ers quarterback and Pro Football Hall of Famer Steve Young, who was on hand for the game in his role as ESPN analyst, said before the kickoff that he figured the 49ers would be conservative with Kaepernick and would lean on his legs and their ground game against Chicago's tough defense. "Don't throw anything you're not sure of," Young said. "It's not the night to try anything. You cannot take this away from your teammates. You can't be the reason they don't have a chance to win. You can't be the reason they lose."

Kaepernick and the 49ers didn't listen. On the third snap of the game, he dropped back and threw a deep ball to his left to Vernon Davis for 22 yards. On the next drive, he lofted a lovely pass to his right to receiver Kyle Williams for 57 yards. That was followed by a three-yard dart to Davis for a touchdown. It quickly became clear that the running quarterback indeed could deliver a deft touch when given the opportunity. He finished the game 16-of-23 for 243 yards and two touchdowns as the 49ers routed Chicago 32–7. On national television Kaepernick not only looked like a starting quarterback, but he also seemed like the quarterback of the future—for the 49ers and for the NFL.

Suddenly, the 49ers had a controversy, though there may not have been much debate at the top of the organization. Smith began to suspect as much when, during the week between the Bears and Saints games, he thought he was ready to pass all of his post-concussion tests, but the team delayed administering them to him. They didn't give him the final one until the Saturday before the game. By then, of course, it was too late. They had to go with Kaepernick. "I wanted this to get cleared and wanted to go," Smith said. "I felt like I was ready. I was fine…I felt like that whole week it kind of dragged on. This protocol of getting back just dragged on and on and on."

Smith said he realized that the concussion protocol that players had to go through to get back on the field was new at that point, and that teams were navigating the procedures for the first time. Still, he came away thinking the 49ers had manipulated the timeline in order to give Kaepernick another start. "It was such a convenient way for them to say, 'We're going to go with Kap,'" he said. "But the concussion stuff also was so gray at that point. It obviously was a touchy subject for everyone in the league."

In New Orleans, a house of horrors for the 49ers in previous years, Kaepernick had another strong outing. He was aggressive and led off the scoring with a seven-yard touchdown run. He finished the day with 231 passing yards, and the 49ers won 31–21. In the days after the game, Harbaugh danced around a barrage of questions as to whether two games were enough for Kaepernick to have bumped Smith aside and become the team's new starting quarterback. He merely said the 49ers were sticking with Kaepernick for now. He had the "hot hand."

Smith never started for the 49ers again. The quarterback, who had rallied the team through the lockout and who had driven it to its first playoff win in nine seasons, had been relegated to the bench without so much as a sit-down meeting explaining the coaching staff's decision. In typical fashion Smith didn't cause a fuss. In fact, he spent as much time at the 49ers training facility as before. But this time he was helping Kaepernick prepare for games. "He was upset obviously that he wasn't playing," Staley said. "But he never became a distraction at all because he could have kind of derailed that and made a big deal about it. He would have had a reason to."

Years later, Smith didn't speak bitterly of how the season played out or have any harsh words for coaches or certainly Kaepernick. But he remembers feeling as if he was on the verge of finally achieving something great for the 49ers—and of making up for all those years of struggle in San Francisco—when he was abruptly given backup duty. "In that system I still had so much growth ahead of me as a player, so much that was untapped," he said. "And I thought I was finally gonna be able to go develop it and become the player I always thought I could be. And I certainly didn't want to do anything to give that opportunity up. Yeah, I knew they had drafted Kap. But I still felt like I could go run with that opportunity and become what I wanted to become and reach my potential and at the same time win a ton of ball games. I was playing the best football—easily the best football—of my career at that point. It still felt like I had so much left ahead of me. So, yeah, that was on my mind at that point. And I also don't think anybody could envision the run Kap went on. I mean, it was historic."

No one in the 49ers locker room begrudged Kaepernick for taking the starting role. He had done nothing wrong. He had simply played well when given the opportunity. Smith had plenty of backers. Staley, the offensive line, Davis, and Frank Gore all were in his corner. But the 49ers were playing so well with Kaepernick at the helm that no one stopped to complain. The team's goal was the Super Bowl, and they were still rolling toward that end. "I don't reconcile anything," Staley said. "It's a team sport, man. I don't reconcile anything at all. I was really excited for Kap and the whole, entire team. And Alex was that same way. I think we were so good that year that we would have gone to the playoffs anyway. But the reason we actually went was because of the offense and what it became that year with Kap running it. It was a perfect time to bring it out because [defenses] really hadn't thought about, figured out how to stop that. But it was pretty crappy how it went down, though because he completely lost his job because of an injury. And they told him to sit. They told him to sit down."

A Wintry Mix

After the road win against the New Orleans Saints, Colin Kaepernick and the San Francisco 49ers lost in overtime to the St. Louis Rams, the team they had tied earlier in the year, then beat the Miami Dolphins at home. If team officials still had any misgivings about installing Kaepernick as their starter at that point, they evaporated the following week, when the 49ers went on the road to play the New England Patriots.

The Patriots were the defending AFC champions, they had won seven straight games entering the meeting with the 49ers, and the game was being aired in primetime. On top of that, the teams would be playing in quintessential New England weather in December: rain, then sleet, then snow, then back to rain—a wintry mix. Kaepernick and the 49ers were undeterred. Despite the nasty conditions, he connected on four of his first five passes on the opening drive, including a 24-yard touchdown to Randy Moss on the sixth play. And they kept pouring it on. The 49ers led 17–3 at halftime and extended the margin to 31–3 in the third quarter on a touchdown throw to Michael Crabtree that threaded three defenders.

That was when Tom Brady and the Patriots woke up. Only one team in NFL history had won a regular-season game after trailing by 28 points. That was the 49ers, who had done it on December 7, 1980 against the Saints, a game they won 38–35. The Patriots looked like they might equal that feat after scoring four touchdowns in the span of a little more than a quarter. After Danny Woodhead scored on a one-yard run and the Patriots converted the point-after attempt with 6:43 in the fourth quarter, the score was tied 31–31. It seemed like it would be another chapter in Brady's multi-volume book of heroics. "It was so cold and so miserable and so rainy that on offense, we were kind of like, 'Okay, let's just run the ball and get it over with,'" Joe Staley said. "Then Tom did four straight touchdown drives—28 points. And it was: *boom, boom, boom, boom*. And before you knew it, it was a tie game."

The 49ers struck back on the next play. Return man LaMichael James took the kickoff back 62 yards. On the following snap, Kaepernick hit Crabtree on a short pass to the left side of the field, the receiver broke a tackle, and ran in for a 38-yard touchdown. The 49ers led the rest of the way, eventually winning 41–34. It was the first time the Patriots had lost at home in December since Brady became the starter, and he had been beaten by a quarterback making his fifth NFL start. If ever there was a signal that Kaepernick was legitimate and that the 49ers were real Super Bowl contenders, this was it. "We can win a shootout," Crabtree, who for years had been reluctant to embrace Smith as his quarterback, gushed afterward. "Whatever it takes, that's our motto…the sky's the limit."

But it also was a costly victory.

The anchor of the 49ers' defensive line, Justin Smith, had entered the game with the third longest starting streak in the NFL. A 12-year veteran at the time, Smith hadn't missed a game since his rookie season with the Cincinnati Bengals. Early in the third quarter, however, he went to stagger his opponent with his left hand—his favorite move—and didn't make contact. "I went to punch him, and he just jumped back thinking that I was gonna bull rush him or whatever," Smith said. "He went back maybe an extra foot, and my arm just whiffed and overextended and snapped. I heard it. I heard it more than felt it."

Smith had torn the triceps tendon on his left arm. As a right defensive tackle, that was the arm he led with, the bludgeon with which he'd initially stun his opponent before trying to move past him with his right arm. The 49ers called it an elbow injury at the time, but it really involved perhaps the most critical muscle when it came to Smith's game. He sat out the following contest against the Seattle Seahawks, a 42–13 blowout defeat in Seattle that would begin a streak of deflating losses there, as well as the regular-season finale against the Arizona Cardinals. The rest didn't allow the arm to heal. He would have to have surgery in the offseason to reattach the muscle to the elbow. Sitting out two games merely ensured he didn't do any more damage before the playoffs began.

Smith was back for the postseason, but he wasn't nearly the dominant, beast-like player who dragged down Drew Brees with one hand and drove Eli Manning into the mud the year before. He estimated the injury cost him 95 percent of the strength in the arm. "It just wasn't as effective," he said. "It didn't have that pop, none of that stuff that you need to have to play. I mean, that was kind of the beginning of my left arm just falling apart. It was my tricep and then my shoulder the following year. That was just the kiss of death for that arm, starting right there."

The 49ers won five of the seven games Kaepernick started in the second half of the 2012 season. They finished the season 11–4–1, earning the No. 2 seed in the playoffs and a first-round bye. Their first postseason opponent ended up being the same one they opened the regular season against, the Green Bay Packers. The matchup meant a return to Northern California for Packers quarterback Aaron Rodgers, whom the 49ers had passed over in favor of Alex Smith in 2005 and who had vowed to make the 49ers pay for rejecting him.

Colin Kaepernick gashes the Green Bay Packers defense for some of his 181 rushing yards. (Terrell Lloyd / San Francisco 49ers)

There also was a bit of mirroring with Rodgers and Kaepernick. Rodgers grew up in Chico, California, rooting for the 49ers and wearing Joe Montana T-shirts under his uniforms. Kaepernick, meanwhile, was born in Milwaukee, raised by devoted Cheeseheads, and likened his improvisational skills to those of former Green Bay quarterback Brett Favre.

Rodgers turned out to be a mere footnote in the second round of the playoffs. The game was entirely about Kaepernick. He began it with a throw to his left that was picked off by Packers cornerback Sam Shields and returned for a touchdown. A year earlier that sort of mistake would have been catastrophic to a cautious, methodical offense that avoided turnovers at all costs. The 2012 version of the 49ers barely blinked at the error. "Even after the pick-six, we were confident," Staley said.

On the ensuing drive, Kaepernick converted two third downs, the second of which was a 45-yard pass to Frank Gore to the Green Bay

22-yard line. Three plays later Kaepernick took a snap out of the shotgun, saw that the left side of the field was clear, and then darted 20 yards for a touchdown. Green Bay's defenders never got a hand on him on the play, which would become the theme of the game. The Packers' edge defenders had no idea how to defend the read-option runs Greg Roman, Kaepernick, and the 49ers threw at them. They never knew whether Kaepernick or Gore had the ball on a given play. Their edge defenders were lucky if they even caught sight of Kaepernick in their peripheral vision as he dashed by.

He ended up rushing for 181 yards on the night. It was the most ever for an NFL quarterback—regular season or postseason—and Kaepernick had done so in his first ever playoff game. Included in that total was a 56-yard run in the third quarter that at the time was the longest run by a quarterback in franchise history. Overlooked at the end of the game was that Kaepernick also had thrown for 263 yards, including two second-quarter touchdowns to Crabtree. That meant he had topped Rodgers, the league's reigning MVP, with his arm, too. Rodgers finished with 257 passing yards and rushed for an additional 28.

The game prompted the Packers coaching staff to head to college campuses in the offseason to figure out how to stop the read-option runs Kaepernick had used so effectively against them. The victory sent the 49ers to the NFC Championship Game for the second straight year. This time it would be played in Atlanta against the Falcons.

Dome Is Where the Heart Is

Most former San Francisco 49ers cite the 2011 divisional playoff win against the New Orleans Saints as their favorite memory of their time with the franchise. For Carlos Rogers it was the NFC Championship Game against the Atlanta Falcons. The 49ers cornerback grew up in Augusta, Georgia, which is about a two-hour drive east on Interstate 20 from Atlanta. His family members always cheered for the teams he was on. But they also were raised as Falcons fans. And everyone—aunts, uncles, grandmas, cousins, more than 30 relatives total—wanted to go to the game. "I remember going over it with my Mom and I'm going, 'What can I do with all these family members? I can't get that many tickets.' So I had to buy me a suite," he said with a chuckle. "I basically spent my whole [game] check on getting my family out there. But that game was real special. It was kind of like how it was for me in college. I played at Auburn, and when I played against Georgia, that was more special to me than playing against Alabama because that was home. Georgia was my home."

On offense the big concern was the sound inside the domed stadium. The 49ers hadn't handled Seattle's crowd noise well in the penultimate game of the regular season. Their 42–13 loss to the Seahawks there had been Jim Harbaugh's most lopsided defeat since he took over as head coach, and the offense twice had been flagged for delay of game in the contest. That was common during the Harbaugh tenure. The 49ers averaged 10 delay-of-game penalties a season during his four years as head coach—by far the most in the NFL. Not only were the team's play calls full of verbiage, but they also had to be relayed from Greg Roman high up in the coaches' booth, to Harbaugh on the sideline, and then to the quarterback in the huddle. At that point he delivered the play to his 10 teammates. On top of that, there were three options on every snap. "We'd have a run that we could change to a pass," tackle Joe Staley said. "And if we got a certain defensive front, we could kill it [and change] to another run. Then we had five other plays that were always options. We could switch to them any time."

Loud venues—especially Seattle's—proved problematic. The 49ers had tried several solutions. They blasted recordings of crowd noise from massive speakers set up around their practice field. No matter how big the speakers were, however, they never could truly duplicate the blanketing din they experienced inside a particularly loud stadium. At one point they passed out plastic ear plugs that were specifically molded to fit each individual player's ears. But those essentially made the players deaf and were unsettling. (Players noted they could hear their own heartbeats when they had them in.)

Heading into the Falcons game, the 49ers decided to turn to another solution: sign language. They had tried using hand signals in Seattle that season and felt they had enough time to augment and perfect that system before going to Atlanta. Instead of screaming out the play calls in the huddle, Colin Kaepernick would sign them. That would both eliminate confusion and allow the 49ers to operate without a huddle. "We put in maybe 80 different hand signals the quarterback had to memorize for all the plays we were going to run," Staley said. "The coaches came up with a language. It might be blunt: open side, weak-side zone. It would be a different play, depending on which hand Kaepernick used to signal. If you go back and watch the film, you can see him doing all this stuff with his hands."

Roman elaborated on the reason for the hand signals. "It was an indoor stadium, the first time Atlanta hosted a game like that, and we knew it was gonna be beyond loud," the offensive coordinator said. "We had a pretty intricate offense, and I wasn't real happy with how long it took to get out of the huddle. So I basically said, 'You know what? Screw it. We're not gonna huddle very much. We're just going to do everything with sign language.' We got some smart dudes up front, and I think they liked it."

Despite all that preparation, nothing worked well at the beginning. The offense began the game with two three-and-out series. The 49ers' defense was even worse. Falcons quarterback Matt Ryan marched his team beyond the 50-yard line on the opening series and then found receiver Julio Jones deep down the left side of the field for a 47-yard touchdown. The Falcons' second drive resulted in a field goal, and on the third, Ryan threw another touchdown pass to Jones down the sideline. This one was a 20-yard score. One play into the second quarter, the Falcons already led 17–0. The home crowd only grew louder. "It was a shock to all of us for us to go down there and play the way we did," Rogers said.

Said Staley: "It was like, 'Holy shit. What's going on here?' And then we just sort of started chopping into the lead."

Atlanta's defense only was marginally better prepared than the Green Bay Packers' had been against the 49ers' read-option runs, and San Francisco's offense started to take advantage in the second quarter. LaMichael James scored on a 15-yard run on the first drive of the quarter. On the second Kaepernick gained 23 yards on a scramble and then hit Vernon Davis on a deep pass down the right sideline to the Atlanta 4-yard line. From there a short Kaepernick-to-Davis touchdown cut the lead to 17–14. "They had no idea what we were doing," Staley said. "I would run at John Abraham like it was a run play, and he'd play it like it was a run. Then they started guessing. Sometimes he'd guess and take himself completely out of the play."

"They didn't know what to do," Roman said. "They weren't going to let Kaepernick keep the ball. They basically said he can't keep the ball, so Gore had a field day. You know that was paradise for Frank."

Gore ran the ball 21 times and finished with 90 yards and two touchdowns. The 49ers' defense, however, still was having just as much trouble as the Falcons' unit. The success of San Francisco's defensive secondary had been built on its ability to bully and intimidate receivers over the middle. But Atlanta had a pair of wideouts, Jones and Roddy White, who wouldn't be pushed around and who were doing plenty of damage along the sidelines. And when Ryan didn't throw to the outside, he found veteran tight end Tony Gonzalez across the middle.

After the 49ers had cut the lead to three, Ryan took over with 1:55 in the half and promptly drove to another score. This one was a 10-yard toss to the middle of the end zone for Gonzalez. When the teams broke for halftime, Ryan already had 271 passing yards and three touchdown passes. Two of them were to Jones, who had 135 receiving yards. One was to Gonzalez, who had caught all five of the passes thrown his direction. The Falcons offense seemed unstoppable.

The 49ers, though, had options. After all, defensive coordinator Vic Fangio had experimented with all sorts of defenses in the run-up to the 2011 season and was good at dialing up specific ones for the opponent. His smart, veteran defense was capable of changing on the fly. And that's exactly what they did at halftime.

Fangio made a subtle yet substantial switch. The 49ers' hard-hitting safeties typically hovered in the middle of the field, putting the corner-backs in one-on-one coverage on the perimeter. Meanwhile, the 49ers' swift linebackers, NaVorro Bowman and especially Patrick Willis, usually were responsible for covering the opponent's tight end. Fangio flipped that in the second half. He had Rogers match up more on Gonzalez. And he had the safeties, Donte Whitner and Dashon Goldson, play more to the outside in order to hold down wideouts Jones and White. The trick was in the disguise. When Ryan glanced at the 49ers' defense before the snap, it looked just like it had in the first half. The defensive backs' assignments, however, had changed. It effectively cooled off the red hot Ryan, whose first drive of the third quarter ended with an interception by cornerback Chris Culliver. "Atlanta didn't have no answers for those changes," Rogers said. "We disguised it well, and Matt Ryan was confused. It's hard for a quarterback to pick out which [defense] we're in when they've got a pass rush coming. You don't have that much time."

Jones, who was on track for one of the most monstrous receiving totals in NFL playoffs history, was held to 47 yards in the second half. Ryan's passer rating, a sterling 151.2 in the first half, was 71.09 in the second. When Gore ran into the end zone from nine yards out—his second score of the half—with 8:27 remaining in the contest, the 49ers had their first lead of the day, 28–24. "I put in some new stuff that we hadn't shown that just torched them," Roman said. "That last touchdown run by Gore was a play we'd never run before. It was a hell of a performance by those guys. I mean, once it was 17–0. After that, man, we just dominated that game."

Atlanta came close to retaking the lead. With his deep options taken away, Ryan led a methodical, 14-play drive all the way to San Francisco's 10-yard line. But on fourth and 4, his pass across the middle to White was broken up by Bowman, whose championship game heroics a year earlier—a would-be forced fumble against the New York Giants—had been taken away by a quick whistle from the officials. This time the 49ers could celebrate. There were no flags on the play. San Francisco took over on downs and a few minutes later were on their way to New Orleans and the franchise's first Super Bowl trip in 18 years.

The team had brought in former owner Eddie DeBartolo Jr. for the occasion, and the 49ers packed into the visitors' locker room for a cramped party. "I remember going to the locker room. It was something you dreamed about as a kid: everyone in there partying with their hats on." Staley said. "The only thing is that I wish it was home that year because that would have been really fun to do that on the field. It was so tiny in there, and you could not move. So I just remember being in my pads forever."

The celebration continued on the plane ride home. Daniel Kilgore, a 24-year-old backup offensive lineman at the time, was from Eastern Tennessee and had asked his buddies, who were planning to attend the game, to come with a little moonshine from his home region. Kilgore snuck a couple of jars of the potent, homemade alcohol onto the plane. "They had brought down flavored apple pie," Kilgore said. "And it's got cinnamon and it's got apples on the bottom of it. So on the plane, we're all celebrating, and I bust out one of those jars of moonshine. And guys are taking little sips of it and saying things like, 'Oh, man, that's good stuff.'"

Because he was a young player, Kilgore sat toward the back of the plane with the rest of the rookies, upstarts, and reserves. The long-time veterans and starters—guys like Rogers, Staley, Gore, and Alex Smith—sat in first class. By the time the little quarts of moonshine made their way to the front of the plane, all the alcohol in them had been consumed. There was nothing left but the apple slices at the bottom of the jar. Alex Smith started munching on those, perhaps unaware of how loaded with alcohol they had become. "Alex eats two of those slices and he's feeling, well, he's feeling pretty good at this point," Kilgore said. "And he was feeling a little frisky."

Smith began to tease the guy across the aisle from him, Rogers, like a big brother would his younger sibling while in the backseat during a long family trip. In fact, he annoyed the cornerback, still giddy about winning a game in front of his extended family, to the point where they started playfully wrestling at the front of the plane. It became the in-flight entertainment: watching the normally mild-mannered Smith, who had always been the adult in the room, have fun in the front of the plane. The rest of the cabin howled with laughter. "That's my boy there," Rogers said with a laugh when asked about the moment. "That's one of the guys I always pulled for even when they pulled him with Kap…I think Alex was just leaning on me so aggressive like being a big child. I was like, 'Alex, move, man!' Maybe that moonshine hit him a little too hard."

After the plane landed, the group of guys partied at a San Jose night-club where a photograph of Smith and Kaepernick celebrating was taken and posted on the gossip site TMZ. A week later, the team was back on a plane to New Orleans, the city where their two-year odyssey had begun.

The HarBowl

The Super Bowl against the Baltimore Ravens began with a 20-yard completion to Vernon Davis…that was wiped away by an illegal formation call against Davis. That opening play set the tone for the disjointed, herky-jerky nature of the game and for a few penalty calls—and non-calls—that didn't go the 49ers' way. "I don't know where that call came from," offensive coordinator Greg Roman said. "They said Crabtree was lined up on the line of scrimmage, but he really wasn't, and it was extremely ticky-tacky. It's unbelievable the guy would call that and do it on the first play of the Super Bowl. It was a big play because we'd have been sitting right around midfield to start the game."

Instead, the 49ers began Super Bowl XLVII with a three-and-out series, the Ravens took over at their own 49-yard line, and then went on a six-play drive that ended with an Anquan Boldin touchdown. For San Francisco the game started like the NFC Championship Game in Atlanta two weeks earlier, but this time the 49ers were adding their own mistakes to the mix. Running back LaMichael James fumbled early in the second quarter, which led to another Baltimore score. On the ensuing 49ers drive, Colin Kaepernick's over-the-middle throw to Randy Moss went over the receiver's head and into the hands of safety Ed Reed. Moss, who was 35 years old at the time and playing in the final game of his career, was criticized afterward for failing to even reach for the ball, but Roman said that on closer examination it was uncatchable. "I don't think he could have in any way, shape, or form affected that pass," he said of Moss. "At first I didn't like it when I saw it live. Then when I went back and I was like, 'Shit, he could have been jumping on a trampoline and still would have had a hard time.' The pass was extraordinarily high."

The next big play came after halftime. Ravens returner Jacoby Jones hauled in the kickoff eight yards deep in his own end zone and then sprinted through the 49ers' kick coverage for a touchdown that gave his team a 28–6 lead. The 49ers and their fans howled that the Ravens held cover man and fullback Bruce Miller on the play—photos show them grabbing handfuls of his red jersey—but there was no whistle. In fact, Jerome Boger's crew called just seven penalties on the day: two on Baltimore and five on the 49ers, including the illegal-formation call on the opening snap.

The 49ers ran three plays on their possession that followed the kick return touchdown. That was when the game became famous for something other than football. The lights went out in the New Orleans Superdome and stayed out for nearly 35 minutes. Elevators suddenly halted, trapping fans inside. Escalators stopped running. So did the coaches' headsets and the television audio feed. No one knew what was happening. It turned out the outage was caused by a newly installed device called a relay that automatically cut power to the stadium when the amperage reached a certain level because the device's factory settings were too low. That was the technical explanation anyway. The Ravens' most recognizable player, linebacker Ray Lewis, had a more insidious theory. He complained the outage was orchestrated by the NFL as a way to allow the 49ers back into the game. After all, they were trailing by 22 points at the time. "You cannot tell me somebody wasn't sitting there, and when they say, 'The Ravens about to blow them out. Man, we better do something,'" Lewis said in 2013. "That's a huge shift in any game in all seriousness. And you see how huge it was because it let them right back in the game."

The 49ers roll their eyes at the theory. They counter that the delay—plus a Super Bowl halftime that is twice as long as that of a normal NFL game—was disruptive for everyone. "I hate that even happened," tackle Joe Staley said. "We had the same delay. Why use that as the excuse for the reason we came back?"

Staley noted that by the end of the season a lot of players were taking painkillers to mask the sprains, strains, and tears they had accumulated during the season. Those painkillers were designed to last the duration of a regular football game. Super Bowl XLVII was decidedly irregular. It ended up lasting four hours and 14 minutes, making it the longest game in Super Bowl history. "My knee, starting in the fourth quarter, started getting creaky," Staley said. "And I was like, 'Oh my God—I'm getting sore right now! This is a five-hour game we're playing.'"

The blackout may have marked the beginning of the 49ers' comeback. The mechanism for it, however, was Lewis. The Ravens linebacker was a 13-time Pro Bowler that year and would go on to be voted into the Pro Football Hall of Fame in his first year of eligibility. He's widely recognized as one of the top inside linebackers to ever play the game. But at the end of the 2012 season, he was a 37 year old at the end of his career who didn't move nearly as well as he used to. And the 49ers took advantage, running their receivers and tight ends on crossing routes in front of the inside linebacker and trying to take advantage of Lewis' lack of mobility in the middle of the field. "He still had great instincts and all that," Roman said. "But athletically and in the passing game, it was tough for him at that point in his career."

Staley was more blunt. "Ray Lewis was out there celebrating after the game," he said. "But he was the reason we were getting so many yards on every play."

Midway through the third quarter, Kaepernick and the 49ers started to roll. On first down from Baltimore's 31-yard line, he threw to his left to Michael Crabtree, who pinballed off of two defenders and ran in for a touchdown. The Ravens' lead was now 28–13. Less than two minutes later, return man Ted Ginn fielded a bouncing ball punt at midfield and got around the Ravens coverage all the way to the Baltimore 20-yard line. That was followed by a 14-yard pass from Kaepernick to Davis and then a six-yard touchdown run by Frank Gore that made the score 28–20 with more than five minutes to go in the third quarter. On that play Delanie Walker, who lined up as an H-back, chopped down Reed with an excellent block at the 3-yard line.

The 49ers defense also woke up after the power outage. On the next Ravens possession, cornerback Tarell Brown knocked the ball from running back Ray Rice at Baltimore's 24-yard line, leading to a David Akers field goal that cut the lead to 28–23. After a Ravens' field goal started the fourth quarter, the 49ers put together a lightning-strike, 76-yard drive that included a long pass to the left sideline to Moss and a 21-yard run by Gore. Two plays after that, Kaepernick set the Super Bowl record for the longest touchdown run by a quarterback when he escaped around the left side of the defense and sprinted into the end zone for a 15-yard score. The 49ers' two-point conversion attempt failed, and it was now 31–29 with more than five minutes to play. The Ravens scored once more in the game. While the 49ers had identified Lewis as the weakness in the Ravens defense, Baltimore seemed to figure out a soft spot in San Francisco's.

During the run-up to the game, it seemed as if nothing would eclipse the Super Bowl's biggest storyline: the two head coaches were brothers. When Jim and John Harbaugh had faced off on Thanksgiving night during the previous season, the brother vs. brother angle had been pumped up to such a degree that even their pregame handshake was filmed and analyzed.

The novelty hadn't worn off by the time they met in the Super Bowl. Every national outlet had a story on the NFL's civil war. Some called it the HarBowl, others the Bro Bowl. Headlines of "Brothers In Arms" were used from coast to coast. Their parents held a press conference during the week. So did the brothers. John was nattily decked out in a black suit with a purple and gray striped tie while Jim wore his everyday uniform: ball cap, black sweatshirt, khaki pants, black socks, and white tennis shoes. They fielded questions for nearly a half hour.

Chris Culliver, however, managed to steal the spotlight. The 49ers' young cornerback had a strong second season in 2012. But his Super Bowl week was awful. The issues began on colorful and chaotic Media

Day when comedian Artie Lange, who was doing interviews for his syndicated radio show, asked Culliver about gay players in the NFL. Culliver took the bait. "I don't do the gay guys, man," he said. "I don't do that."

Lange then asked if he thought there were any gay players on the 49ers. "No, we don't got no gay people on the team," Culliver said. "They gotta get up out of here if they do. Can't be with that sweet stuff. Nah…can't be…in the locker room, man. Nah." Finally, Lange asked if gay players would have to keep their orientation a secret. "Yeah, come out 10 years later after that," the cornerback said.

Lange played the recording on his radio show that night, and it created a media firestorm for Culliver and his teammates both in New Orleans and back in the Bay Area. The 49ers said they rejected the cornerback's views and Culliver apologized and later agreed to undergo sensitivity training. Still, it became the biggest storyline that week for the thousands of reporters who were on hand to cover the Super Bowl. And Culliver's daily media sessions were dominated by the topic.

During the game the Ravens seemed to take advantage of Culliver's rough week. Quarterback Joe Flacco targeted him nine times, and 123 of Flacco's 287 passing yards that day came on throws in Culliver's direction. That included a 56-yard touchdown to Jones in the second quarter, in which Culliver was beaten deep, overran Jones as the receiver caught the ball and fell to the ground, and then couldn't make the tackle after Jones got to his feet and sprinted the rest of the way for a touchdown.

The Ravens continued to pick on him on their late fourth-quarter possession. Flacco threw in Culliver's direction on third and long to open the drive, drawing a pass-interference penalty on the cornerback that resulted in a first down. The Ravens eventually moved the ball to San Francisco's 20 where Justin Tucker booted in a short field goal to make the score 34–29 with 4:19 left to play.

The 49ers took over at their own 20-yard line needing a length-of-field touchdown drive like the one they had had against the New Orleans

Saints a year earlier. The momentum clearly had swung to their side, and it seemed as if they would get it. On their fourth play, Kaepernick again went in Crabtree's direction as he flashed across the middle of the field for 24 yards. Crabtree finished the game with five catches for 109 yards. On the next play, Gore picked up big blocks by Staley, left guard Mike Iupati, Miller, and Walker and rumbled 33 yards all the way to the Ravens 7-yard line where he was driven out of bounds.

The 49ers had been blasting through Baltimore's defense since the power outage and now were a mere seven yards—with a first down, two timeouts, and the two-minute warning to work with—from taking their first lead in the Super Bowl. "We were standing there with first and goal and were all looking at each other and were like, 'We're going to have a fucking parade! We're about to be Super Bowl champions! This is so cool!'" Staley said. "We thought 100 percent we're scoring. The way we were playing on offense, especially with the offensive line that we had, we thought we were going to run the ball in."

Gore's long run, however, set in motion a series of unfavorable circumstances for the 49ers. It meant that he was winded and had to come off the field for the first-down play. Gore was the team's best short-yardage runner. Indeed, he may have been the best short-yardage runner in the NFL at the time with an uncanny ability to root out extra yards even when there was little room to run. As he jogged to the sideline on first and goal, James was sent in for a snap. "And LaMichael James is down in there, and I'm going, 'Oh, shit,'" Roman said, "because he had fumbled earlier in the game and he wasn't a very good runner up the middle. So that kind of caught me off guard at the time, but it is what it is. And their linebacker—Ellerbe—made a really good play."

Dannell Ellerbe stopped James after a two-yard gain. If the 49ers had reached the 3-yard line, Roman said he likely would have tried to pound the ball into the end zone on the team's next three plays. The 5-yard line, however, was too far to go against a defense intent on plugging the run.

So he called a pass play on second down, one in which Kaepernick rolled right and tried to hit Crabtree in the near corner of the end zone. The receiver was well-covered, and his throw fell incomplete.

Then it was third down from the 5-yard line. The Ravens were expecting a pass and were in a split safety look. They had only seven men around the line of scrimmage. Knowing he would go for it on fourth down, Roman gambled and called a quarterback run, thinking it would catch the Ravens off guard. That's exactly what happened. Kaepernick took the ball out of the shotgun and started heading left. Tight ends Davis and Walker were lined up in front of him, and right guard Alex Boone had pulled in that direction. Gore essentially was the quarterback's lead blocker. The numbers were in the 49ers' favor. "It was quarterback power. We had the play. We all blocked the play," Staley said. "And it was a walk-in touchdown."

The 49ers could practically feel the cold metal of the Lombardi Trophy in their hands. There was just one problem. The play clock was fast approaching zero, and Jim Harbaugh started signaling for a timeout just before the ball was snapped. It was granted, the whistle blew, and the play was halted as Kaepernick was making his move to the line of scrimmage.

It was the worst possible scenario. Not only was a probable, go-ahead touchdown wiped out because the play had been stopped so late, but the 49ers also had revealed their plan of attack. The element of surprise now was gone. "The problem from my perspective was that we ran that play, and they saw it," Roman said. "They got to see the play we're running to win the Super Bowl with. And as soon as that happened, I knew immediately that they were going to all-out blitz us to stop the run, and that we would have to probably throw it in because it'd be 11 dudes up around the ball. I knew when that happened that we were going to have to do with Colin what was his greatest weakness, which was throwing the ball in the tight red zone. So I had a seminal moment right there, shall we say. He's walking into the end zone, the play's whistled dead, and I'm thinking to myself, *We're going to be getting all-out blitzed* and *Do you really want to end the Super Bowl running the ball into an all-out blitz right now?* You can't. It's stupid. It's absolutely stupid. If you can do third-grade math, you know that."

So the final two snaps were pass plays to the same receiver, Crabtree, toward the right side of the end zone. On third down Crabtree lined up in the backfield and then sprinted down the line of scrimmage to the right. Kaepernick hit him in stride, but the play was diagnosed well by the Ravens, and two defensive backs, Corey Graham and Jimmy Smith, blasted Crabtree short of the goal line, and the ball was incomplete.

Then it was fourth down, the 49ers' last chance. Kaepernick had two receivers to his left and Crabtree to his right. The receiver had a one-on-one matchup with Smith, who at 6'2", 210 pounds was big for a cornerback and who was known for his physical style of play. With their safeties inched up toward the line of scrimmage, the Ravens sent an all-out blitz at Kaepernick, and Ellerbe immediately shot through a gap in the offensive line. With the linebacker bearing down on him, Kaepernick had to rush his throw, and the ball to Crabtree in the corner of the end zone went well over the receiver's head. Jim Harbaugh, Crabtree, and the entire 49ers sideline screamed for a holding or a pass-interference call on Smith, who had held up Crabtree in the end zone. "There's no question in my mind that there was a hold on Crabtree on the last play," said Jim Harbaugh, who had thrown his hat in disgust and who was demonstrably pantomiming a holding signal after the play.

"He was definitely being held," Roman said. "And in the normal course of most games, that's going to get called. The only question there…was it a catchable ball?" Their cries fell on deaf ears. The officials had called just seven penalties and weren't about to call their eighth at such a critical moment. There was no yellow handkerchief to save the day, and the 49ers' last real shot at a Super Bowl title had fallen five yards short.

There was still 1:46 to play. But San Francisco had only one timeout remaining—another consequence from the near play-clock violation, and the Ravens effectively salted away the game. "I was super, super pissed," Staley said. "I threw my helmet on the ground, and it just exploded. Someone yelled, 'We've still got a chance!' And I was like, 'Fuck it. It's over.'…[I] balled my eyes out in the locker room with [Offensive Line Coach] Solari. He hugged me like a baby. I was like, 'I'm so sorry!' And he said something like, 'Don't be sorry. You did everything you could.' And I said, 'It hurts so bad!'"

CBS wanted Jim Harbaugh to talk outside the losers' locker room after the game was over. He said he wouldn't do it. None of the team's star players—Patrick Willis, NaVorro Bowman, Davis, and Gore—were in any condition to speak on national television either. They were all in tears, slumped inside their own lockers, and with towels covering their faces. Center Jonathan Goodwin was the only one composed enough for the job. "We really felt the year before we should have won," said Staley, Goodwin's linemate. "And we didn't. And we felt we were robbed that we didn't have it. So it had become, 'This is the year we were going to win it.' And to come so close and then not come away with it—it was extra emotional for all of those guys."

CHAPTER 9
SHERMAN VS. CRABTREE

The story of the San Francisco 49ers' 2013 season begins at a softball tournament in Arizona. Larry Fitzgerald, the prolific Arizona Cardinals receiver, holds a charity game in Scottsdale each year and invites other NFL players to take part. One of the players invited in the spring of 2013 was 49ers wideout Michael Crabtree. Another was Seahawks cornerback Richard Sherman. By 2013 Crabtree was one of the better receivers in the league. He finished with 1,105 receiving yards in the just-completed season, becoming the first 49ers pass catcher since Terrell Owens in 2003 to break the 1,000-yard mark. He'd had big games against Arizona's Patrick Peterson and all of the top cornerbacks in the league—except for one. "Some people just match up better in certain things," Sherman said of covering Crabtree. "You know how certain teams match up better? The same thing's true with certain players. I was just a good matchup against him. I didn't feel threatened by him in any capacity."

Crabtree wasn't on hand for the softball game itself, but he showed up for the cocktail party in the evening that's held in the pool area of the W hotel. Everyone was dressed nicely, were sipping drinks, and were engaged in conversation. Sherman said he was talking with another 49ers receiver, Kyle Williams, who had played at nearby Arizona State. "Me and Kyle are friends and we were having a conversation about the season," Sherman said. "In the offseason we don't take it as serious as everybody thinks. Guys aren't sitting there—well, most guys—aren't sitting there, 'Oh, you play for the other team? Hmmmm.' When we line up in a game, it's, 'Hey, I'm gonna try to kill you for the next 60 minutes.' Once that's over we'll shake hands, and it's, 'I'm glad you didn't get hurt. Now go home to your family.'"

At that point Crabtree joined the group but didn't stick to the good-natured script everyone else was on. He pointedly informed Sherman that he was going to get the better of him in the upcoming season. "It was like, 'Hey, this year I'm going off on you. I'm going for 150 [yards] two [touchdowns]. You better watch it,'" Sherman said. "And I'm like, 'Cool, brother. Easier said than done. Good luck with that. I'll see you in September, and we'll do the dance.'"

The back and forth ended with Sherman thinking it was odd behavior for a charity event, but that it was over. It wasn't. Later in the evening, Crabtree approached him again, and Sherman said this time he was even more aggressive. "Now it's not football anymore, and now you're acting like you want to fight," Sherman said. "And then he started to say some things that I'm just not going to put on the record because it's not worth it. But it was just way more personal and way more confrontational, and I'm a pro, you know what I mean? And we're at a charity event. I have a ton of, a ton of—tons—of respect for Fitz, so I never, ever in my wildest dreams would do anything crazy on a trip like that. It would be embarrassing."

Instead, Sherman tucked away the anger and rage that Crabtree had incited and saved it for a later date. It doesn't take much to motivate Sherman, who joined the 49ers in 2018. Inside his head he turns seemingly the smallest slights—a quarterback saying he's not afraid to throw to Sherman's side of the field, for example—into something outrageous and blasphemous, something he can feed off in the week leading up to the game and during it. His confrontation with Crabtree was real and it was personal. And Sherman nurtured the memory of it throughout the offseason. It was something Sherman wouldn't forget or forgive. "So I'm like, 'All right, brother. Let me tell you this: we play twice a year, and for as many years as you play in San Francisco, I'm going to embarrass you,'" Sherman said. "'We can handle all this—this animosity that you have and everything that you're feeling—on the field. And I promise you, I'm going to beyond match your energy and I'm going to go beyond what you're feeling right now. I'm going to try to embarrass you every single chance I get.'"

A Collision Course

If 2011, Jim Harbaugh's first season with the San Francisco 49ers, was the fun year, and Year Two was the business-like year, then Year Three was about toil. The veteran 49ers knew—could feel—that their window of opportunity for winning a Super Bowl was closing. As much as that, having played deep into the postseason the two previous years and doing so with punishing practices along the way had started to take its toll. The 49ers entered the 2013 season with a weight on their backs. "It had a different feel that year," tackle Joe Staley said. "People started getting egos, and the coaches are talking different, and the players are acting different. Stuff that was fine to deal with the first couple of years, now guys were like, 'Why are we still doing this?'"

As the season began, the team reasoned that it had become so battle-tested over the previous years that it was capable of winning a playoff game—or three or four of them—on the road. The 49ers were willing to sacrifice some regular-season wins and perhaps even a division title if it meant being fresher when the playoffs began in January. "That was kind of the internal struggle a little bit," CEO Jed York said. "It was: should we try to get guys healthy? Or do you play everybody and try to win and have the best record that you possibly can, but the guys might not be healthy for January? And that was always kind of the give and take that year. And I think there was always a feeling that that team could go anywhere and beat anybody, that we did not have to be the home team to win with those guys. That team was such a professional team, and they were ready to rock and roll. And the other thing was that you knew that you were playing Seattle one way or the other."

The 49ers weren't exactly on fire to begin 2013. By mid-November they were 6–4 and dueling with the Arizona Cardinals for second place in the NFC West behind the Seattle Seahawks. Still, they did what successful, seasoned teams do late in the year. They focused, won their final six games, and earned the NFC's fifth seed in the playoffs. The Seahawks were the No. 1 seed, which meant the road to the Super Bowl would go through Seattle. It was San Francisco's lowest seeding since Harbaugh had arrived. It didn't matter—at least not initially.

The first two playoff games that January certainly weren't easy. But there was an air of inevitability among the 49ers that they would meet the Seahawks in the championship game. The opening games of the postseason—it made no difference who the opponent was—merely were the warm-up act for what everyone understood would be the main event, the true Super Bowl that year.

The 49ers' wild-card round game on January 5, 2014, was played in a polar vortex that swallowed Green Bay, Wisconsin, and the midsection of the country and plunged temperatures to below zero degrees by game's end. The weather was a massive storyline going into the contest, and there was all sorts of fretting and analysis about how a California team would fare in the frigid upper Midwest. It turned out to be a nonstory. Colin Kaepernick, whose family is from Wisconsin, signaled the 49ers would be undaunted by coming out with bare arms, throwing for 227 yards, and rushing for another 98 yards against the team he had throttled in the playoffs a year earlier. "It's not that cold. It's all mental," he said afterward.

Staley wasn't bothered by it either. "We basically had a jet-engine flame thrower on the sideline," he said. "I love playing in the cold because you don't sweat, and you get so much warming stuff on the sidelines so you don't actually notice the cold."

The road game against the Green Bay Packers should have been tense. The widest margin throughout was six points. The 49ers lost a lead early in the fourth quarter, regained it on a 28-yard throw from Kaepernick to Vernon Davis, and then watched as Green Bay's Mason Crosby made it 20–20 with a 24-yard field goal with a little more than five minutes to play. The 49ers, however, felt like they were in control throughout.

When Kaepernick got the ball back after Crosby's field goal, he led a methodical, 13-play drive that left veteran kicker Phil Dawson, who had been the first player to emerge from the tunnel and examine the frozen field that afternoon, with a 33-yard game-winning attempt with three seconds to play. "That was Colin Kaepernick at his best," Greg Roman said. "He had a great, winning performance. The game [against the Packers] in '12 was freakish. But to go up there in the cold weather on the road—I mean, it was freaking freezing—and he just managed that game so well. He used his legs. He played a very mature game. You know, the year before we just had beaten them in a historic way. But Dom Capers made a bunch of adjustments on defense, and they were playing a bunch of cover zero. So we had to kind of adjust on the fly. And I thought Kaepernick just played his ass off in that game. It was just really a smart game."

Dawson nailed his kick, the game was over, and the 49ers celebrated, though not too much. "That was actually a really weird game because it was a close game the whole time, but there was a really weird calm on the sideline. There was no tension. Even after the game, too, it was like," Staley said, shrugging his shoulders, "'We won.' There was no crazy jubilation like we had after the Saints game where everyone was so physically and emotionally spent. It was like, 'We won the game. Good job, Phil. Way to kick the field goal.'"

There was a similar atmosphere the following week in Carolina. The 49ers had lost 10–9 to the Panthers earlier in the season. But when it came to the playoffs, the 49ers were battle-hardened. The game in Charlotte, North Carolina, was their seventh postseason affair in three years. The Panthers were the new kids. And they acted like it. They chirped, strutted, beat their chests, and pressed their facemasks into the 49ers' after big plays. The over-the-top bravado was met with a yawn from the San Francisco players. Harbaugh often would warn them not to get "emotionally hijacked" by the situation. There were no hijackings taking place on the 49ers' sideline or huddle. Meanwhile, the Panthers had two unnecessary roughness penalties and another for unsportsman-like conduct. "They were acting crazy," Staley said. "We were laughing at them. We were telling them, 'You guys aren't even ready for this yet. You don't know how to act.'"

The 49ers pulled away in the second half and won easily 23–10. Ahmad Brooks, an outside linebacker, lined up on the inside on a goal-line play and at one point leaped over both the offensive and defensive lines like a comic book hero. Kaepernick scored on a four-yard run and afterward struck a Superman pose—the one Panthers quarterback Cam Newton liked to do—by pretending to unbutton his shirt and reveal the "S" underneath. The win, however, set up an encounter with their arch nemesis, the Seahawks, in a building that had become Kryptonite to the 49ers.

House of Pain

The rivalry had begun years earlier when Seattle Seahawks coach Pete Carroll was at USC, and Jim Harbaugh was the coach at Stanford. At that time USC was one of the nation's most dominant programs. With the ever-churning Harbaugh pumping it full of confidence, Stanford was the upstart eager to knock the Trojans from their perch. And Harbaugh and Stanford prominently did so in 2007 when they upset the No. 2-ranked Trojans 24–23.

Harbaugh delighted in being a thorn in Carroll's side from that point forth, including two years later when Stanford walloped USC 55–21. Included in that score was a late, two-point conversion by Stanford that

Carroll saw as rubbing it in. It led to a testy postgame exchange at midfield. "What's your deal?" Carroll famously asked Harbaugh.

By 2013, however, the roles had been reversed. Harbaugh's San Francisco 49ers had won the NFC West the previous two seasons and had gone to the Super Bowl in 2012. Carroll's young, aggressive Seahawks were practically foaming at the mouth to replace them at the top of the division. The 49ers won both meetings in 2011. From that point forward, it was clear the Seahawks were catching up quickly.

The 49ers won home games against Seattle in the 2012 and 2013 regular seasons, but the margin was becoming increasingly narrow. Meanwhile, the games in Seattle's raucous and ridiculously loud CenturyLink Field had become laughably one-sided in favor of the home team. The scores were 42–13 in 2012 and 29–3 in Week Two of the 2013 regular season. "I just didn't want to play in Seattle again," Joe Staley said about the playoff game there. Offensive coordinator Greg Roman had an even more candid take. "Quite frankly, they were just better than us. Yeah, I had to invent shit just to give us a chance, basically."

The 49ers not only had been blown out when they went to Seattle, but a San Francisco team that prided itself on its might and toughness also had been battered. Tight end Delanie Walker broke his jaw there in 2011, receiver Mario Manningham suffered ACL and PCL tears in a loss in the same 2012 game in which tight end Vernon Davis was given a concussion when he was blasted out of bounds by safety Kam Chancellor, who was easily the most menacing Seahawks player of them all.

During the Week Two loss in Seattle in 2013, Colin Kaepernick was injured when a Seahawks player landed on his foot, causing a chipped bone and a ruptured capsule in the ball of the foot. He couldn't push off or accelerate like usual, and both his rushing numbers and passing statistics suffered until the injury healed later in the season. After that, Kaepernick, who'd set a quarterback rushing record in the 2012 playoffs, didn't have more than 20 rushing yards in a game until a Week Seven win against the Tennessee Titans. "Kaepernick got a lot of heat on social media," Roman said. "And he was playing with a broken foot, just gutting through it. And I think he took a lot of that stuff to heart because his numbers were down, blah blah blah. He's such a social media guy, always reading what they said. And I think it really kind of scarred him a little bit. *Here I am, I've got a broken foot. I'm gutting through it. I can't tell anybody, and all these people are doing is ripping me.* That kind of thing. And honestly that's kind of when I first started noticing a little bit of change in him."

The goriest injuries in Seattle were still to come. Early on in the 2013 NFC Championship Game, the 49ers offensive linemen were seated on the bench when left guard Mike Iupati looked over at his linemate Staley and was startled to see blood all over the tackle's uniform. "Where are you bleeding?" Iupati asked.

Staley had dislocated his thumb in the second quarter and had run over to the sideline to have the team doctor jam it back into place. It worked, but it had been done with Staley's glove still on his hand, which masked the severity of the issue. The left tackle not only had suffered a dislocation, but it also had been a compound dislocation, which meant the bone had ripped through the skin. Staley's glove had filled with blood over the next few plays, and it finally had come gushing out on the sideline. "I looked down at my hand, and my glove had pooled with blood and was flowing down my arm," Staley said. "I took the glove off, and it was like mangled. It was shredded. It was so disgusting."

The injury happened before halftime. Doctors stitched up Staley's thumb in the locker room and then gave him a numbing agent that made it feel as if he were swinging a rubber mallet the rest of the game. Some of the stitches opened up, but Staley didn't know or care. He couldn't feel anything from the third quarter onward. The injury never became public afterward because he missed only one kneel-down snap before halftime and because the 49ers would go on to suffer even more horrific injuries throughout the game.

Iupati, who had been particularly effective against the Carolina Panthers a week earlier and who had been selected to the Pro Bowl that season, broke a bone in his leg on a short touchdown in the second quarter and missed the rest of the game. Then in the fourth quarter, the 49ers suffered the most gruesome injury of all. The score was 20–17 in favor of the Seahawks at that point, and Kaepernick had just lost a fumble that the Seahawks returned to San Francisco's 6-yard line. The noise inside the stadium had been deafening since pre-game player introductions. After the takeaway it became so loud that there was almost an absence of sound. It was pandemonium.

The Seahawks and their fans smelled blood and sensed victory. If they took that momentum and scored a short touchdown, the game would be over. They'd have toppled the mighty 49ers once and for all and they'd be on their way to the Super Bowl. The 49ers, meanwhile, realized their only hope was a valiant defensive stand. And it appeared that would happen when linebacker NaVorro Bowman stopped receiver Jermaine Kearse at the 1-yard line on third and goal and then ripped the ball free from the receiver and tucked it into his own arm. Bowman, whose forced fumble against the New York Giants two years earlier had been taken away and who had knocked away the Falcons' last-ditch effort in Atlanta in the 2012 NFC Championship Game, had done it again.

The play, however, wasn't over. Teammate Eric Reid arrived and accidentally drove Kearse into the side of Bowman's leg, which was planted firmly on the ground. The angle and the impact essentially ripped the linebacker's lower left leg from his upper leg at the knee. Bowman suffered a multi-ligament tear that would require extensive rehabilitation and cause him to miss the entire 2014 season. "I could hear him yelling," teammate Patrick Willis said afterward. "I never heard him yell like that."

Bowman was still hanging onto the ball as he fell to the ground in agony and was clearly touched down by a Seahawks player. But in his distress, he eventually released the ball, and the Seahawks gathered it in. At the time loose ball scrambles couldn't be reviewed on replay—the rule would be changed a few months later—and despite Bowman's sacrifice and heroic effort, the Seahawks were awarded the ball at the 1-yard line. "Y'all robbed me, then made a rule about it," Bowman said years later about the controversial play.

"You knew that game was the game," Jed York said. "I will put that up as one of the most physical games that's ever been played. I mean, our guys gave everything. Bo literally gave everything, and our D stepped up and played their hearts out. And you know, it was just two awesome teams and two immovable objects running into each other."

Maybe there was some sort of higher power that had watched Bowman's injury unfold and didn't like the unfair outcome as far as which team was awarded the ball. On the ensuing fourth-down play, karma struck. The Seahawks flubbed the snap, and the 49ers gathered in the bouncing ball at their own 15-yard line.

Two plays later there was another wild swing when Chancellor intercepted Kaepernick's pass at San Francisco's 40-yard line. The Seahawks turned that gift into a 47-yard field goal and a 23–17 lead. At that point there only was 3:37 remaining. Entering the game, Roman knew he had to do something different to generate yards against a Seattle defense that had held opponents to 10 or fewer points seven times during the regular season. "That defense Seattle had in 2013 was legit," Roman said. "I mean, we all saw what they did the next week to Denver in the Super Bowl. That's one of the top five defenses of the last 25 years."

Roman and the 49ers decided that their best chance was to use the Seahawks' aggressiveness against them. They figured out how Seattle's defensive line liked to rush Kaepernick and where the escape hatches would be for evacuating the pocket. They called fake handoffs, on which

Kaepernick would keep the ball and then have a lead blocker in front of him. Roman was particularly proud of a delayed draw, in which the team's pass catchers—Frank Gore from the backfield, Michael Crabtree, and Davis—would take off from the line of scrimmage as if they were on pass patterns. In reality, they were assigned to be downfield blockers for Kaepernick. Roman called the specially designed play twice. Kaepernick gained 58 yards, the longest play for either team that day, on one of them to take the 49ers to the Seattle 10-yard line in the second quarter. It set up San Francisco's first touchdown of the game, a one-yard plunge by Anthony Dixon.

Kaepernick finished the contest with 130 rushing yards, the third-highest total of his career. "Basically, everything looked like one of our deep, play-action passes that we run, but instead of running routes, guys were actually running to block people," Roman said. "And [the Seahawks] were pretty predictable with how they play defense, so we kind of knew what their adjustments would be. So I think later after the Seahawks watched the game, they were like, 'Oh my god, they weren't even running routes. They were actually running downfield to block.'"

That was the backdrop of the final drive. At 23–17 a field goal was useless. A touchdown would win it. After three plays the 49ers were facing fourth and 2 when Kaepernick hit Gore down the left sideline for 17 yards that got the 49ers to their own 47-yard line. Three snaps after that, Kaepernick again went to his left. This time he connected with Crabtree for 16 yards. On the next play, he found Davis across the middle for 11 yards. Suddenly, the 49ers were on Seattle's 18-yard line with 30 seconds remaining.

On the other side of the field, Richard Sherman was disgusted. The man who had vowed to upstage—no, to embarrass—Crabtree after their offseason encounter in Arizona hadn't been given any opportunities. There had been one throw in his direction early in the second quarter, and that had been wiped out by a holding penalty on Sherman. Other than that,

In a physical NFC Championship Game against the Seattle Seahawks, wide receiver Michael Crabtree would play a pivotal role. (Terrell Lloyd / San Francisco 49ers)

the Seattle cornerback hadn't even been targeted. The 49ers were marching down the field, and Sherman, who had asserted himself as the NFL's top cornerback that year, wouldn't get an opportunity to stop his rivals. He felt like a mere observer. "I'm like, 'I can't believe this,'" Sherman said. "The clock's going down. They're walking it down the field. They're about to score, and I've got nothing. It was like, I'm watching from the stands. I'm watching, and it's like they're not even going to give me a shot."

But with 30 seconds left, Sherman lined up in his usual spot on the left side of the defense and finally found Crabtree staring at him from the other side of the line of scrimmage. In fact, he was the only 49ers pass catcher on Sherman's side of the field. Everyone else was lined up to Kaepernick's left. At the snap Crabtree shuffled his feet as if he was going to run a hitch route, one in which the receiver takes a step back toward the quarterback for a short completion. It was meant to draw Sherman forward, but Crabtree didn't sell it hard enough. "It was actually a double move," Roman said. "And you really couldn't tell by watching it."

Sherman certainly didn't fall for the ruse. "As he stuttered, I'm thinking to myself, *There's no reason to stutter. You're not running a hitch. You're not in a position to run a hitch. That's not the play y'all need*," the cornerback said. "So I'm like, 'Okay, I'm not breaking on a hitch.' And as he did that, I was like, 'I'm gonna keep up. I'm going to keep moving down the field.'"

The play was designed to go to the deep, right corner of the end zone. Defensive end Cliff Avril, however, got a good rush against 49ers right tackle Anthony Davis and forced Kaepernick to hurry his throw. Crabtree, meanwhile, never broke free of Sherman, who had sealed off the receiver as the ball was launched into the air. Sherman remembers two things happening at that point. The first is that he momentarily lost the ball in the lights as he positioned himself for an interception. "And now I'm blinded from looking at the light, so I can't see it," he said. "But I'm dialed into where it should be. And I'm just starting to refocus back and I'm going up to get it."

The second is that Crabtree knew the defender was in a better position for the ball and gave Sherman a shove in the back hoping that it would sail past his foe and into his hands for what would have been a game-winning touchdown for the 49ers. "As I'm going up, I feel somebody push me in the back and I'm like, 'There's no fucking way'—excuse my language—there's no way he's going to get away with this PI,'" Sherman said. "I thought I was gonna pick it. And it was going to be an easy pick and I'm ready, I'm right there. And when he pushes me, I'm like, 'This is a PI, but they're never gonna call it because the playoffs. Nobody's ever going to call it.'"

After being shoved in the back, Sherman had to take a step forward. At that point he knew he wouldn't be able to grab the ball with two hands, but he realized he still could reach the descending ball with his trailing hand and try to bat it back toward a teammate. That was something he and the other Seahawks defensive backs had fooled around with in practice that season, getting the scout-team quarterback to make throws just outside the boundary of the end zone so they could rehearse leaping up and tipping the ball back in bounds to a teammate.

It had worked earlier in the season in a road win against the Giants. In practices Carroll allowed the talented defensive backs to mess around with the play but warned them about outsmarting themselves and batting the ball back to an opponent for a touchdown. Usually, in those practice scenarios, the ball ended up in the hands of Earl Thomas or one of the other Seahawks safeties. This time it wound up going to speedy linebacker Malcolm Smith, who was trailing on the play. Sherman said he didn't know that at the time. "I just saw color. I didn't know who it was," Sherman said. "I knew it wasn't a 49er. I knew it was a blue jersey. I just didn't know who it was."

Sherman was on the ground when he fully realized who had the ball and what that meant for the outcome. Then he put his hands in the air and began celebrating with teammates. He did more than that, running up to a dejected Crabtree, giving him a facetious slap on the butt, and then getting in his face. After that he flashed a choke sign at Kaepernick, who had shown the audacity of attacking Sherman at such a critical juncture of the game.

The cornerback was only starting to wind up. He had to be dragged to the Seattle sideline as the Seahawks offense went through its final kneeldowns to end the game. Then he had an emotionally charged interview with FOX sideline reporter Erin Andrews in which he hinted—with explosive anger—at the charity event confrontation with Crabtree. Of course, no one knew what he was talking about at the time, including Andrews. Sherman had held onto the memory and stoked it throughout the season. He finally unleashed the burning animus he had been keeping inside since the spring. "I'm the best corner in the game! When you try me with a sorry receiver like Crabtree, that's the result you're going to get! Don't you ever talk about me!" He boomed.

"Who was talking about you?" Andrews asked.

"Crabtree! Don't you open your mouth about the best, or I'll shut it for you real quick. LOB!"

All of that occurred on camera, but there's an unknown postscript to the epic battle between the Seahawks and 49ers that day. The tunnel from CenturyLink Field leads to the home and visiting locker rooms. And between them is a small space for family members to gather after games while players are dressing and doing their postgame interviews. Jed York and his younger brother, Tony, were stationed in that area after the NFC Championship Game. So was Sherman's older brother, Branton, who is just as good as Richard at getting under others' skin. In fact, Branton serves as Sherman's biggest motivator during the course of a season, pointing out slights that Richard has received on social media and elsewhere and otherwise making sure the sizable chip Richard carries on his shoulder never diminishes. "He's an instigator about me and to me," Richard said. "My brother will get me riled up. 'Oh, you can't do that, you can't jump that fence, or you can't cover that guy, or you can't stop that guy. Man, that guy's gonna kill you on Sunday.' But he's also my biggest supporter, so he won't let anybody else say anything bad about me."

Tony York, meanwhile, had a fiery temperament of his own. And when Branton started hitting on Tony's girlfriend after the game, the two came very close to trading blows. Their brothers—who four years later would become employer and employee—had to rush in and break up the fight. "His brother was super keyed up that night," Jed York said. "He was hitting on my brother's girlfriend. And then Tony got into it with Sherm's brother. Then I came over, and Sherm came over, and, whatever, they got separated. But it got a little heated. There was a lot of emotion on every side after that game."

"We were trying to separate them," Richard Sherman said of the incident. "But once you become peacemakers and it's your brother, you've gotta pick a side, and brothers are brothers. It doesn't matter how old you are or how young you are. You're picking your brother's side."

York and Sherman didn't discuss the scuffle when the cornerback signed a three-year contract in 2018. But York did bring it up at a service for Tony York, who took his own life at age 35 in December of that year. At first, Sherman didn't know how to react to Jed talking about the altercation on such a solemn occasion. But he soon realized he wanted to laugh about the charged moment and remember the big personality that his little brother had.

A year after Tony York's death in a road game against the New Orleans Saints, the 49ers wore helmet decals with "TY" on them. It was the most emotional game of the year—similar in frenetic pace to the team's epic win against the Saints in the 2011 playoffs. After the 48–46 victory in 2019, coach Kyle Shanahan presented gameballs to the York family— one each for parents, Denise DeBartolo and John York, and all of Tony's siblings, Jenna, Mara, and Jed. "We talk about everyone being family," Shanahan said in the visiting locker room in New Orleans. "You say it on a lot of teams, man. But as we've known all year, it's different here. And it starts with these guys."

CHAPTER 10
A MORE DYNAMIC DUO

The end-zone interception that Richard Sherman caused was an arrow through the heart of the Jim Harbaugh-era San Francisco 49ers. They played decently the next season—the team finished 8–8—but the hunger, gleam, and feistiness that were so prominent in 2011 had faded as 2014 drew to a close. The 49ers were like Sisyphus, straining to push a mighty boulder to the top of a hill each season—only to have it go tumbling to the bottom in the final leg. In 2014 they only could move it halfway up.

Four years earlier Harbaugh and general manager Trent Baalke had sat next to one another at Harbaugh's introductory press conference at the swanky Palace Hotel in San Francisco. It was a triumphant moment for Baalke, who was starting his first season as the 49ers' general manager. The two men had hit it off during a secret meeting in January of 2011 at a time when the Miami Dolphins and a host of other NFL and college teams were clamoring to hire Harbaugh away from Stanford. Baalke's ability to reel in Harbaugh—as well as what looked to be an excellent 2011 draft class—won him the NFL's Executive of the Year that season.

They were buddies, copilots, and racquet ball adversaries during their first season together. During the 2011 draft, Harbaugh's first in the NFL, he gushed about how Baalke ran the draft room, saying he was a "steely-eyed missile man" at the helm. Their relationship was off to a smashing start. But it wasn't long until cracks started appearing. Harbaugh and Baalke not only stopped appearing in any more joint press conferences after that point, but they also were rarely seen together in public. As is often the case in head coach/general manager dynamics, a massive tug of war had begun over control of the team, which players to bring in, and how they should be managed and developed. There were no knock-down, drag-out sessions. It became more like a Cold War between the two excessively controlling personalities with each man retiring to his side of the organization and then drawing a curtain to keep the other out.

The dysfunction was easy to detect. "The first year we were there we were two special teams plays away from playing for the championship," cornerback Carlos Rogers said. "The second year we played for the championship. The third year we played Seattle, and they were a tough team, too, but we were still another game away from going to the Super Bowl. With that team we had, it would have been great to get another opportunity with that group. I think egos got in the way. I don't think Trent and Coach Harbaugh got along. As a matter of fact, I know they didn't. During that second year, we would come across Harbaugh all angry like, 'Man, they got rid of my player. I could develop this guy, and they didn't even tell me,'" Rogers said. "And I was just like, 'What type of relationship y'all got?'"

The coaches on Harbaugh's staff felt that during the 2014 season the 49ers' front office was eager to torpedo Harbaugh's chances and did so by weaponizing the injured reserve list. The coaches figured they'd only have to wait a certain amount of time before a player returned from injury. Once the front office placed that player on injured reserve, however, his season was over.

Former and current team officials deny that was the case. They say that three deep trips into the postseason—plus Harbaugh's demanding style—simply began to take their toll on the roster. "When you have three long seasons and you don't have a championship to show for it—yeah, it just wears on you," the team's CEO, Jed York, said. "And it's really, really hard to be able to go back to the NFC Championship Game after you lose a Super Bowl and then lose in that fashion in that game [in Seattle]. It was tough."

Whatever the reason, the 49ers roster had started to come apart at the seams. When the 2014 season ended, there were 20 players on one injury list or another, including inside linebacker Patrick Willis, center Daniel Kilgore, and first-round draft choice Jimmie Ward. Linebacker

NaVorro Bowman didn't play a snap that year. Defensive tackle Justin Smith's left arm still didn't feel right.

York decided he couldn't continue with a head coach and general manager who didn't speak with one another. And at some point during the 2014 campaign, he made a choice between the two: Harbaugh would have to go. At season's end the 49ers issued a statement that said the parting was "mutual," which Harbaugh would later say wasn't the case. He said he was told in mid-December that he wouldn't be back and that he coached the last two games knowing he'd be gone. The 49ers won the finale against the Arizona Cardinals 20–17, a victory that players seemed to deliver for the outgoing coach. That brought Harbaugh's four-year record to 49–22–1. "I count up these wins. That's 49 wins," Harbaugh said in his final appearance as a member of the 49ers. "That seems appropriate."

The 49ers not only had missed the playoffs in eight seasons before his arrival, but they had been a laughingstock for much of that period. Harbaugh and his talented staff immediately turned them into a fearsome contender and led them to the NFC Championship Game over the next three seasons before falling to .500 in his fourth. "And then Harbaugh gets the blame for it," Rogers said. "That's what I hate about GMs. Ya'll bring in all these players, but then the coaches get the blame for them when they don't pan out."

Joe Staley reflected on Harbaugh's final season with the 49ers. "[It] was a really weird year," tackle Joe Staley said. "I remember reading things like, 'Harbaugh on the hot seat' and 'Things are not going well.' And as players you're like, 'We just came off of three straight NFC championships. How much better can it get?'"

Both new coaches the 49ers hired—Jim Tomsula in 2015 and Chip Kelly a year later—were doomed to fail. So was Baalke. The quality, tough-guy players brought in by Mike Nolan and Scot McCloughan during the previous decade steadily were leaving the roster. Quarterback

Alex Smith was traded to the Kansas City Chiefs before the 2013 season. Willis retired following the 2014 season. So did Justin Smith, whose left arm never was the same after the triceps tear he suffered in 2012. After sitting out the entire 2014 season, Bowman never fully recovered from his grisly knee injury. Talented pass rusher Aldon Smith, whom Baalke had drafted in the first round in 2011, was arrested in August of 2015—his third on suspicion of drunk driving since entering the NFL. After the last arrest, he was booted from the team. That represented a huge blow to Baalke, who had become close to Smith and who had vouched for him during his many transgressions.

Baalke, meanwhile, struggled to regenerate the roster. It was like Terry Donahue's 2004 missteps were occurring all over again. Baalke, for instance, thought a player he drafted, running back Carlos Hyde, could replace aging Frank Gore beginning in 2015. He couldn't. In fact, despite Gore being in his 30s and Hyde being in the prime of his career, the older player outrushed the younger one 2,953 yards to 2,396 yards over the next three seasons. That was a theme after the 2014 season: all the great players the 49ers lost were replaced with lesser reproductions. And by the end of the 2016 season, the 49ers had descended back to their terrible 1978 and 2004 states—talentless, rudderless, and having won just two games. They were once again in need of a total reboot.

At that point York's top criterion was finding a head coach and a general manager who not only could work together, but who also actually liked one another. "The whole thing was we wanted to have a coach and GM be able to come in together and know that they're a team and they're fighting together and they're going to go through this stuff together," he said, "because I had just seen it where talent at some point doesn't overcome weaknesses in your organizational structure."

At first the 49ers zeroed in on a pair of New England Patriots: offensive coordinator Josh McDaniels and director of player personnel Nick Caserio. The two had played on the same team at John Carroll

University. Caserio had beaten out McDaniels at quarterback, causing McDaniels to move to receiver and giving the former teammates the kind of background and longtime working relationship York wanted as the foundation of his team. When it became clear the 49ers wouldn't be able to pry the duo from the Patriots, York moved on to another top target, then-Atlanta Falcons offensive coordinator Kyle Shanahan.

The 49ers had pursued Shanahan two years earlier, hoping he would serve as Tomsula's offensive coordinator. Shanahan and a host of other candidates had turned down the job. "It was the agent at the time who was kind of putting out fairly negative things like [Shanahan] would never come here," York said. "And Kyle was the one who actually reached out to me. And he was like, 'Hey, man, I just want you to know I committed somewhere else. And I committed a while ago. I walked out of Cleveland. I needed to make a decision for my career and I know Dan [Quinn]. I've connected with him and I feel like this is a better opportunity. And I have all the respect in the world for 49ers.' And he was one of the only people that has ever reached out in a way like that. So I always had a lot of respect for him, and that's sort of where our relationship started."

When the two reconnected two years later, York felt like the fit was perfect. He liked that Shanahan had been laser-focused on being part of the NFL since he was a young boy. He liked that the Falcons assistant was widely considered one of the top offensive minds in the league. And he also liked that his career to that point hadn't been entirely smooth. Shanahan had been criticized for his handling of quarterback Robert Griffin III when Shanahan was the Washington Redskins' offensive coordinator. He had desperately—and successfully—gotten out of his contract after one year with the Cleveland Browns. And despite the roaring success Atlanta's offense had in 2016, Shanahan bore the brunt of the blame for the team blowing a 28–3 third-quarter lead to the Patriots in the Super Bowl. York felt all of that ultimately would make him a more-seasoned—and better—head coach. "Kyle ran into things as a coordinator that most people don't deal with," he said. "And it might look like it's a bad thing at the time, but I think it helped build his character."

Shanahan's family connections didn't hurt either. His father, Mike, had been the 49ers' offensive coordinator for three seasons in the early 1990s, the last of them culminating with the franchise's fifth Super Bowl victory at the end of the 1994 season. That glorious season, as well as a love for all things 49ers, became imprinted on Kyle, who was a 15 year old at nearby Saratoga High School at the time. He said he received a throwback Deion Sanders jersey for Christmas in 1994 and then wore it every day for the next month. "I was dedicated," Shanahan said. "I felt like I couldn't do school for that month because I had to get a good night's sleep before the games and things like that. I was just so, 100 percent the Niners and the playoffs at that time. I can remember it like it was yesterday. I remember people making fun of me because I got Deion Sanders' throwback jersey for Christmas and I didn't take it off until the day after the Super Bowl until my dad became the Broncos' head coach. So I wore it for about a month and 10 days. I changed my undershirt, though, I promise."

When the Shanahans moved to Denver in the winter of 1995, Mike brought the 49ers' ideology with him. Mike had coached in San Francisco under George Seifert, who had been alongside Bill Walsh since 1977 when they were both at Stanford. That meant that Mike Shanahan was part of Walsh's storied coaching tree. And when he went to Denver, anyone could see the similarities in the teams' offenses and operations.

His son was taking notes the entire time.

On game days Kyle was a mere step away from his father. He was the guy who made sure the head coach's communications cords—there were no WiFi connections for talking to the assistants in the coaches' booth back then—never became snarled on the sideline. During the spring and summer, Mike allowed Kyle, who was an elite high school receiver at the time, to bring his football buddies to the Broncos practice facility so that they could train alongside Terrell Davis, Ed McCaffrey, Rod Smith, and the other Broncos players. Teenaged Kyle Shanahan would run routes against the Broncos defensive backs. They were well aware he was the head coach's son. But they didn't go lightly on him. "Billy Jenkins hit me in the face so hard my mouth started gushing blood on the field," Shanahan said. "I tried to hold it together out there, then I went inside and didn't want to show my face. It was so embarrassing. My dad wouldn't have it. He made me go out there, and I had to walk around with a busted-up face."

The time spent at the Broncos facility—in the training room, on the practice field, just shooting the breeze between sessions—taught Shanahan the patter of an NFL facility. He learned how to talk trash, pull pranks, and carry himself around a professional facility. He also realized how serious these men were about their craft, how easily they sniffed out frauds and fakers, and concluded that if he was going to become an NFL head coach, he had to be the sharpest guy in the room. Having his father's last name would only get him so far. "I knew what I was getting into," he said. "That's why I worked so hard and stuff. I wanted to make sure I did know what I was talking about. If you ever get around a group of NFL guys and you don't know what you're talking about, I can't imagine how insecure you'd be because it's at a very high level. It's very intense, and that's why I never wanted to get into coaching until I absolutely knew that I put in the work, I put in the hours. I never wanted a player to ask me something I couldn't help them with. Knowing what their expectations were before I got into it was what helped me be so ready."

That was the background Shanahan brought to his meeting with York in January of 2017. "And when we sat down, it was very clear that we saw a football organization in a very similar way because it all stemmed from Bill Walsh," York said. "So we fit very well."

But who would be Shanahan's partner atop the team's football organization? There wasn't an obvious connection like McDaniels had with Caserio in New England. The 49ers interviewed nine candidates in January of 2017, including Minnesota Vikings assistant general manager George Paton and Cardinals executive Terry McDonough. The team liked all of the prospects, but the relationship had to be perfect. And neither Shanahan nor York felt as if they had found Mr. Right.

From TV to GM

While the San Francisco 49ers were conducting their general manager interviews, John Lynch was high up in a television booth providing Sunday analysis for FOX Sports. Lynch had been a safety for 15 seasons, his last full year coming in 2007. He had been voted to nine Pro Bowls and had won a Super Bowl with the Tampa Bay Buccaneers. The Stanford product was a brainy brawler, who was smart enough to run Tampa Bay's—and later on the Denver Broncos—secondary while also carrying a reputation as a punishing hitter.

In January of 2017, he was the color commentator on FOX's No. 2 broadcast team. Joe Buck and Troy Aikman would get the top game each week in places like Dallas or Green Bay. Lynch and his play-by-play partner, Kevin Burkhardt, often found themselves calling Atlanta Falcons games because Atlanta was good that season—11–5—but not necessarily the most popular team on television. As an analyst Lynch had production meetings with coaches and coordinators a few days before their games. One of his favorites was Kyle Shanahan. Lynch had played for Mike Shanahan in Denver, and he and Kyle also had been with the Buccaneers at different times and could talk about their shared acquaintances in that organization. Mostly, Lynch enjoyed the Xs and Os conversations he had with the young offensive coordinator and gushed over what he saw on the field on Sundays. "I was thoroughly impressed," Lynch said. "There are guys who impress you, and there are guys who, it's like, 'This guy's different, the way he calls offensive football, the way he sees things, the way he sets up his run game.' Looking at it as a defensive player, you're going, 'That would be really hard to defend.'"

Lynch and Burkhardt called a divisional-round playoff game in January that year, a 36–20 win by the Falcons against the Seattle Seahawks. Shanahan's offense rolled up 422 yards of offense against one of the best defenses in the league. Lynch knew Shanahan was being considered for head coaching jobs at the time and during the broadcast he gave Shanahan a vote of confidence on the air. "I said, 'If I'm an owner out there, what are you waiting for?'" Lynch said. "'This guy's showing everything he needs to show.' And he may be prickly—I forget the words I used, but it was something like that—and I said, 'What are you waiting for? Go hire this guy.'"

A few minutes later, Lynch's phone buzzed in the broadcast booth. It was a text message from Jed York. It read: "I'm trying to!"

"I don't know where he got my number; I've never asked him that," Lynch said. "I saw [the phone] buzz, but I couldn't look at it then because it's the middle of the game. And after the game, I'm checking my texts and I respond back, 'Trying to do what?' And he writes back: 'Trying to hire Kyle.'"

At that point Lynch hadn't thought about joining the 49ers' front office. He was close with Broncos general manager John Elway, who had once asked him to do some scouting-type analysis on defensive backs. Lynch enjoyed the exercise, figuring that someday he might like to be the general manager of an NFL team like his buddy, Elway. But he never really pursued the idea. After all, he had a great, high-salary, low-stress job with FOX. His family, including four kids, were set up in his hometown of San Diego. Perhaps he'd have been interested in being a general manager if the Chargers had stuck around that city and they had an opening at the top of their front office. But in mid-January of 2017, Lynch was content to be where he was.

That changed a few days after the Falcons' division round win when he gave Shanahan a congratulatory phone call. "And I just said, 'Hey, I want to tell you, I thought that gameplan was masterful. Everything we talked about—I saw it come to fruition on the field,'" Lynch said of the conversation. "And I said, 'It looks like you've got a good shot at this San Fran job. I don't know if that's the one you want, but it looks like that's promising.' And he kind of shared with me that, 'Yeah, that's the one I've kind of got my eye on.' And we talked about it, and then, almost as a throwaway line, he kind of said, 'I'm frustrated because I can't find a GM that I really want to work with. And I think that's really important.' And I didn't know if he was just saying it because it was on his mind or saying it [to ask] if I knew anyone because he knew I was out and about. So I just said something like, 'Well, I'll keep my eyes and ears open' or something like that. And I hung up."

That night Lynch had trouble sleeping. In fact, he couldn't sleep for the next four nights. He was restless. He was fidgeting. His season was over, so he was supposed to relax. But he wasn't at ease. His mind was racing, and one morning he realized why. "I woke up one day and I said, 'I know what it is. It's what Kyle said,'" Lynch said. "And so, my wife said—at the time we'd been together 23, 24 years—'I know what you're like when you get like this. You better do something right away because I can't live with you when you're like this.' So I called Kyle and just said something like, 'Hey, man, you said something the other night, and it's been gnawing at me.' And then I said, ''What about me?'"

Shanahan's first reaction was to question why Lynch would ever want to leave his current job, which is considered one of the plum assignments in the NFL world. It paid exceptionally well, provided the football fix that all former stars crave, and also allowed Lynch to spend most of the week—and all of the seven-month offseason—with his wife and kids. Shanahan first wanted to make sure Lynch knew what he might be stepping into. "And he said, 'You understand the work, right?'" Lynch said. "And I said, 'Yeah, I think I do. I've watched Elway operate in it over the years and I'd be interested.'"

Shanahan considered the proposal and a few days later called Lynch back. "He said, 'Hey, this dude named Jed's gonna call you,'" Lynch said with a laugh. "And so I said, 'Yeah, I know who Jed is.' And so Jed called and he said that Kyle's really interested, that he didn't know if Kyle was going to be the guy, but that it was trending towards that and would I be interested in flying up there if he sent a plane down."

The next day Lynch was having dinner with York and his wife, Danielle, at their Los Altos Hills home. He spent the night, and the next day York, team president Paraag Marathe, and Lynch were on a flight to Atlanta to meet with Shanahan. The dinner the night before was more of a get-to-know-you session. The flight east served as Lynch's job interview. "Then we got there with Kyle, and it was like, 'Holy cow! This whole thing is speeding up now. Now I've got a decision to make,'" Lynch said, "because Kyle basically said, 'This is the guy I want to work with. And If you guys can figure it out and if you want to do it, John, I would love to work with you.' And at that point, Jed said, 'I'm all for it,' and told me the job is basically yours if you want it."

Lynch's instincts were screaming at him to take the offer, but his brain still was trying to catch up. It had only been days—hours really—since he had first broached the subject with Shanahan. There was his family to consider. (In fact, he was due to attend a father-daughter dance in San Diego that evening.) He and FOX were in talks about a new contract. There had been some flirtations from other networks, including about getting him on the Thursday night primetime broadcasts.

General manager John Lynch and head coach Kyle Shanahan have formed a tight bond atop the 49ers organization. (Terrell Lloyd / San Francisco 49ers)

He also thought there was an assumption by the 49ers brass that he and Shanahan had known each other for years and were longtime buddies. That really wasn't the case. "It was interesting," Lynch said. "There was a perception—even with Jed—that we knew each other a lot better than we did. But I just know that sometimes you have that with people where there's a connection when you talk. And when we first started talking, it was, 'Hey, what do you think the two most important things are when building a football team?' And my answer was: 'We gotta find our quarterback and we gotta find the d line.' And [Shanahan's] like, 'Dude, I totally believe in that.' And it went on from there. Everything kept aligning. There was a point that was really powerful in that meeting where Jed said, 'Okay, I'm going to leave you two because you have to figure out who would have [control of] the 53 [man roster], who's got the draft, who's got this and that. And Paraag and I are going to get out of here.' And I said, 'Wait. Why do you guys need to leave? We're all going to be working together. Kyle and I are comfortable together. Let's sit here and talk it out.' And so we did, and everything just had a very nice fit. It felt right."

If Lynch kept glancing at his watch, it wasn't because he didn't enjoy the company. He had a date with his daughter he absolutely had to keep. He told York, Marathe, and Shanahan that he had to talk to his family, but that he'd make his decision quickly. Then he was back on the private plane to San Diego. He was shamefully late to the dance, but he had a couple of accomplices working on the inside to make sure it didn't end without him. "Philip Rivers—his kids went to school with my kids," Lynch said of the veteran quarterback. "God bless him, he kept tipping the DJ to keep the party going so that I could get one dance because I texted. I said, 'Guys, I'm five minutes out. Is it still going on?' And Mike Sweeney, another pro athlete [a former All-Star with the Kansas City Royals,] was there and he's like, 'Philip's giving the guy hundreds left and right to try to keep the thing open!' And so I ended up making it for one dance. So it was cool."

York and the 49ers had gone through almost the entire month of January without finding the right person to be their general manager. They told Lynch he was their top candidate, but that he had only 48 hours to decide if he wanted the job. The answer, of course, was that he did, and on January 29—a week before Shanahan was set to coach in the Super Bowl—the team hired Lynch as its new general manager.

York and the 49ers loved Lynch's reputation around the league—not only as a brutally hard-hitting safety, but also as an analyst for FOX. He was smart. He was handsome—perfect for being the face of the franchise—and well-liked. When he attends the NFL Scouting Combine in Indianapolis each year, Lynch can't walk 10 steps without having someone stop him and shake his hand or ask to take a picture. And while he never lost his ultra-competitive spirit, Lynch also didn't arrive with an oversized ego, which York appreciated.

Lynch knew he'd never served in any front office—much less as a general manager of a professional team. He knew he didn't know everything and he immediately surrounded himself with experienced personnel executives like Martin Mayhew, a longtime cornerback who had served as the Detroit Lions' general manager, and Adam Peters, whom Lynch was able to hire away from the Broncos and whom Lynch installed as the 49ers' vice president of player personnel. "The great thing about John is he didn't want to come in and be the football czar and make every single decision," York said. "He knew that there was a lot that he needed to learn and that he needed to lean on people. So when you bring up somebody like Adam Peters that he was able to bring in, it was very similar when we hired Scot [McCloughan in 2005]. If Scot had had a John Lynch figure on top of him, it would have been a very, very different scenario in my opinion, and I think it would have helped Scot kind of grow in that role. So it was just—it was nice to have guys that put ego aside and who just said, 'This is how we build a team, and we need to figure out how to supplement where we're weak.' And that's where John was really, really forthcoming in terms of like, 'I want to be great, but I know I need help being great.'"

CHAPTER 11
THE JOKER, JIMMY G, AND A REVAMPED D

Kyle Shanahan and John Lynch officially took over the two-win San Francisco 49ers in February of 2017 and quickly determined there were only a few things worth saving. Whereas Jim Tomsula and Chip Kelly were given little opportunity to revamp the roster during their respective seasons as head coach, Lynch and Shanahan had license to do what they wanted. They weren't dainty about the process. To them the 49ers' roster was a near tear-down situation. Three years after they took over, the only incumbents remaining on offense were left tackle Joe Staley and running back Raheem Mostert. There were a few more on defense, including defensive tackle DeForest Buckner and safety Jaquiski Tartt. Other than that, Shanahan and Lynch decided they needed to lay down an entirely new foundation for the rebuilding 49ers.

Their first few moves weren't exactly home runs.

Shortly after free agency began, they held a press conference to introduce seven veteran newcomers. They included the 49ers' new starting quarterback, Brian Hoyer, who had spent a season playing under Shanahan with the Cleveland Browns. Hoyer already had been in the league for eight seasons and never had a real chance to become a team's starting quarterback. He had that in San Francisco, and early on it looked as if he would seize the opportunity Shanahan was giving him. He looked excellent in spring and summer practices, showing a strong command of the offense and a connection with his receivers, especially on throws deep down the field. When the season began, however, Hoyer seemed to shrink. He completed just 58 percent of his passes in his first six starts, all of them losses. Midway through his sixth start, he was pulled in favor of a rookie, C.J. Beathard.

Hoyer largely symbolized Shanahan's and Lynch's initial free-agent class. Linebacker Malcolm Smith tore a pectoral muscle in training camp, sat out the entire season, and never caught on in two-and-a-half years. Receiver Pierre Garcon suffered a neck injury, missed half the season, and would go on to score just one touchdown in two years with the team. Another receiver, Marquise Goodwin, was brilliant in his first year in San Francisco but was a non-factor in the next two. There were more misses than hits, and some were very expensive whiffs. The same was true of Shanahan and Lynch's first draft.

The 49ers had the No. 2 overall selection that April and swapped it for the No. 3 pick, adding three additional picks in the process. It initially was seen as a coup by the team's new front office. The 49ers took the player they would have nabbed at No. 2, Stanford defensive lineman Solomon Thomas, and used the extra picks to jump back into the first round for the top linebacker in the draft, Alabama's Reuben Foster. Lynch may have been a first-time general manager, but he already looked like a genius. And his first draft was hailed as a rousing success.

A year and a half later, however, no one was praising the team's draft day maneuvers. Thomas, who wasn't big enough to be an impactful defensive tackle nor quick enough to be a full-time defensive end, appeared more like a backup.

Foster was much, much worse. After joining the 49ers, he was arrested on three separate occasions, including after an extraordinarily messy incident involving his on-again, off-again girlfriend at his home in Monte Sereno, California. Following the third arrest—involving the same girlfriend at the team hotel before a 2018 game in Tampa, Florida—the 49ers had seen enough and released him on the spot. The 49ers lost 27–9 to the Tampa Bay Buccaneers the day after the incident. It marked the low point of the season and of the Shanahan-Lynch regime.

A rebuild would be impossible if the new sections Shanahan and Lynch were adding either never got off the ground or resulted in a spectacular collapse. That was the outside perception at least. Inside team headquarters a quiet confidence was building that everything was heading in the right direction despite a string of losses to start the 2017 season and some conspicuous missteps when it came to gathering talent. For one thing, Shanahan and Lynch also hit on some of their draft picks—even if they didn't know it at the time.

While they were evaluating Beathard before the 2017 draft, for example, Iowa's tight end kept popping up on the game film. George Kittle was a late bloomer. He had been a receiver in high school. When he arrived at Iowa, he had the right height to be a tight end, but his body had yet to fill out. He weighed around 200 pounds. Was he a big receiver? A tight end? Should the Hawkeyes try to convert him to defensive end? No one knew. Those closest to Kittle back then described him as "gangly." He looked like a scarecrow. He received one of Iowa's last scholarship offers in 2012, and no one there thought he'd amount to much. Most of the coaches, in fact, had never heard of him. Five years later, he was still filling out his frame.

And that wasn't only one of the things going against him at the time of the draft. Another was that he played at Iowa, a team with a throwback offense that's devoted to run blocking but one that doesn't put the ball in the air very often. Kittle had excellent speed for a tight end, but he hardly got to show it off in college. During his final season at Iowa, he caught 22 passes for 314 yards and four touchdowns. Those are fine numbers, but they certainly didn't grab anyone's attention.

Finally, Kittle had a reputation for being gregarious. Perhaps too gregarious. "He really enjoyed his redshirt year to the point where, somewhere around the building, he was classified as a social butterfly, life of the party," Iowa's offensive coordinator at the time, Greg Davis, recalled. "To the point where I called him in and I said, 'George, you really have a gift. You can really run, you'll be a matchup nightmare, and you are tough. But are you really serious about being a great football player?'"

Kittle doesn't dispute his reputation. He partied too hard and drank too much when he first arrived in Iowa City. It's something he realized early in 2015. During the TaxSlayer Bowl, the Hawkeyes were being blown out by Tennessee, and there wasn't a thing Kittle could do about

Known for his outsized personality, tight end George Kittle gets set during the 49ers' NFC Championship Game victory. (Kym Fortino / San Francisco 49ers)

it. He was a redshirt sophomore at that point, but he was buried so deeply on Iowa's depth chart that a freshman was inserted into the game ahead of him. None of the coaches took Kittle seriously. He later had a long talk with the school's assistant strength coach, Pat Angerer, who had played linebacker at Iowa, had been drafted by the Indianapolis Colts in the second round, and had played in the NFL for four seasons before rejoining his alma mater. Angerer also had been a hard partier, who hadn't done much during his freshmen and sophomore seasons. Before his junior year, however, he woke up—and sobered up—and became a star by the time his senior year ended. "I asked him, 'What did you do?'" Kittle told *The Washington Post.* "He said, 'I stopped drinking so much. I stopped going out so much. I stopped fighting people when I got drunk and focused on football.' I said, 'Well, I'll do the same thing.' I didn't really fight anybody, but I changed all that up. And I am where I am."

The constant partying at Iowa ceased, but the party-boy label stuck with Kittle and made it into the NFL draft reports. Perhaps that's why Kittle, who ran like gazelle and was one of the more vicious and relentless blockers among tight ends in the 2017 draft, dropped all the way to the fifth round. "There were some things being said about George, that football wasn't everything, which is so ironic," Lynch said. "But it was that—and I don't want to make this into a big deal—but that he was a little bit of a frat party guy."

Still, the 49ers loved what they saw on film. Shanahan needed a capable blocker at tight end for the outside zone runs that are such a staple of his offense and he figured a guy with Kittle's speed—only two tight ends were faster at the NFL Scouting Combine that year—might become a decent pass catcher, too. They put a third-round grade on him, which is where tight ends coach Jon Embree hoped the team would take Kittle. The problem was that the rebuilding 49ers had a lot of needs, and tight end wasn't at the top of the list. Early in the third round, they selected a cornerback, Ahkello Witherspoon. Later in the day, they made a trade to jump back into the end of the third round, but it was to take Kittle's Iowa teammate—and roommate—Beathard. In the fourth round, the 49ers drafted one of Shanahan's favorite running backs, Utah's Joe Williams. When the fifth round began, the 49ers couldn't believe that two of their favorites, Kittle and Louisiana Tech receiver Trent Taylor, remained on the board and they ended up taking both in that round. "I always joke that we didn't draft [Kittle] until the fifth round, so we weren't that smart about it," Lynch said. "But we did have him tagged as someone we liked."

When the fifth-round tight end arrived, the 49ers found someone smart, irreverent, and with boundless energy. Kittle never shuts off, never slows down. When he was a red-shirt freshman at Iowa, he was limited to the scout team, which meant his only job that season was to get the starters ready to play their upcoming opponent. Kittle made the most of that bit role, taking trips to the local arts and crafts store each week and doctoring his helmet and jersey so that it looked like that of the Hawkeyes' next foe. If it was Michigan, he took a roll of yellow masking tape and skillfully recreated the Wolverines' helmet. If it was Nebraska, he covered his helmet with two rolls of cream white tape and punctuated it with a red "N." The rambunctious freshman took his part so seriously that it sometimes led to on-field scuffles with the older players, who were upset the skinny freshman was being so rough in the practice sessions. "It was fun going against those guys every day," Kittle said in a 2018 interview with The Athletic. "And whenever you put a good block on them, they'd swing on you and try to fight you and tell you not to go so hard and stuff like that."

Kittle excels at getting under others' skin. He has a skill for it. With the 49ers he turned into the locker-room rascal, constantly playing pranks on teammates like switching the clothes hanging in one player's locker with those of another. On another occasion he arrived at a post-game press conference wearing a T-shirt that was emblazoned with a picture of shirtless teammate Jimmy Garoppolo. Kittle is the 49ers' joker. In fact, the tight end had exactly that— Heath Ledger's Joker character—tattooed on the inside of his left arm early in 2019. That's just one of his personas. "He acts like a WWE wrestler, and I don't think that's an act," Shanahan said. "That's who he is 24/7, which is fun to watch. But you've always got to watch out for him. He's pretty rowdy all the time."

Building a Super Bowl Team

Kyle Shanahan's first season as head coach didn't begin well as the San Francisco 49ers got off to an 0–9 start. But the type of players he and John Lynch brought in signaled to some of the longest-tenured veterans that the team was on the right path. Joe Staley, for instance, played on some terrible teams when he first entered the NFL in 2007. Then he was part of the quick rise to the top under Jim Harbaugh. After that he watched the 49ers descend again under Jim Tomsula and Chip Kelly. He knew what a winning team looked like—and more importantly, what it felt like—and he had a sense that things would change despite the ugly start.

Staley saw promise in players like George Kittle and Trent Taylor. He immediately could tell that free-agent fullback Kyle Juszczyk was an excellent acquisition. After the 49ers traded for guard Laken Tomlinson just before the regular season began, Staley took the new offensive lineman under his wing. Despite being thrown into the mix at the last minute, Tomlinson was playing next to Staley by the second game of the season and has started every 49ers game from that point forth.

Even in someone like Solomon Thomas, who has frustrated fans since he was selected with the third overall draft pick, Staley saw a bright, team-oriented player and a tireless worker. Over more than a decade in the NFL, the veteran left tackle had learned that those qualities were more crucial than raw talent as far as building the foundation of a team. "Everybody looks at a guy like Solomon Thomas and says he's not a home run," Staley said. "That guy works his ass off every single day. You know exactly what you're going to get from him. Those are the kinds of things that build quality franchises. Bringing in guys like that spoke to what [Shanahan and Lynch] thought was important. I think it's more about the character and what you're getting every single day and someone you can count on to be the guy who's going to show up and give you everything he has…They're not all going to be home runs. But if you keep bringing quality people in, you're eventually going to build a roster that goes to the Super Bowl."

The Super Bowl? In 2017 a return to the big game in the near future seemed farfetched. The 49ers' 0–9 start was their worst in franchise history. Even the miserable 1978, 2004, and 2016 squads had notched a win earlier than Shanahan's inaugural team. Of those nine losses, however, five came by three or fewer points. That told the 49ers they were close to breaking through. Players also said that Shanahan did a masterful job of nudging them along and showing them they were improving. His offensive scheme wasn't easy to pick up. It required practice and precision, and the young head coach kept telling his players how much sharper, how much better they were becoming each week. "Kyle did such a great job in meetings of showing us a play that we had run early in the season and then showing us running that same play later in the season," Juszczyk said. "And so we could see how we were improving. We were getting better. There was improvement being made. It just wasn't showing on the scoreboard."

The breakthrough finally came in Week 10 against the New York Giants. The theme of the game was resilience and staring down adversity. And it was personified in wideout Marquise Goodwin. When the contest began, Goodwin had been awake for two days. His wife had gone into premature labor the day before, and the couple had lost their son early on November 12, mere hours before the game against the Giants was set to kick off.

The couple was devastated and cried together. But at some point that morning, Goodwin said his wife, Morgan, urged him to join his teammates and take part in the game. He not only suited up that day, but also delivered the 49ers' biggest play of the season. The team was trailing 6–3 in the second quarter of what had been a dull and slow game to that point. On third and 8 from his own 17-yard line, C.J. Beathard dropped back, looked up, and then launched a ball deep down the middle of the field to Goodwin, who had gotten past Giants cornerback Janoris Jenkins. The ball dropped into the receiver's hands at New York's 36-yard line and Goodwin, a former track star at the University of Texas, sped away from Jenkins for an 83-yard touchdown, his first true explosive score of the season. As he was coasting in, Goodwin pointed toward the sky in a gesture to his infant son. Then he dropped to his knees in the end zone before finally falling forward under the weight of his emotions.

Goodwin's touchdown was a thunderclap. It seemed to awaken the 49ers, who were a different team from that point forward. Later in the game, tight end Garrett Celek broke loose for a 47-yard catch-and-run touchdown, Beathard had an 11-yard touchdown run, and running back Matt Breida, an undrafted rookie that season, scored from 33 yards out. When time expired the 49ers had 31 points, the Giants had 21, and Shanahan had his first victory as the 49ers head coach. "We've done some explosive things this year, but we haven't gotten any explosive touchdowns," Shanahan said after the game. "It was just nice today to get one, not only that play [by Goodwin] but the one to Celek and the one to Breida. It just felt real nice to see some of those explosive guys making a hell of a play and finishing for points."

The 49ers were essentially a new team. They'd only been playing together for a couple of months. But the celebration afterward was one you'd expect from guys who had been together for nearly a decade and who had finally won something momentous like a championship. The locker-room party was emotionally charged. The 49ers were celebrating for each other, for Shanahan, and because they truly wanted a team that was going about its rebuilding project the right way to be successful. The win against the Giants was reassurance that the 49ers could be— would be—winners. "We genuinely care for one another and we wanted to show that this group together could be something special," Juszczyk said. "And to show that in order to succeed, you don't have to be miserable and just grind, grind, grind. You can enjoy your teammates and your relationships but also work and have success. It was crazy. At 0–9 we still came in to work happy. It wasn't a miserable place to be at all. And that came from Kyle and his consistency, not being up one day and down the other, and him doing such a good job of showing us we were improving."

"We had been so close on some of those losses," cornerback Ahkello Witherspoon said. "That taste of victory was so close so often that when we finally got it—that's why it felt so sweet. That moment was so awesome."

Said Staley: "It was getting that first win, of course. But it was even more exuberant than that. We really believed in Kyle and John and all the hard work we put in. Having as much adversity as we had at the start of the season and the fact that no one was pointing fingers—to finally get that monkey off their backs, I was happy for them. I think that's why the celebration was so wild."

The winning didn't stop there. Two games later Jimmy Garoppolo, whom the 49ers had acquired in a trade with the New England Patriots, made his first start in his new red and gold uniform in his hometown of Chicago. He looked like the second coming of Brett Favre, continually pulling rabbits out of his hat at critical moments, particularly on third downs. His favorite target was Taylor, the 5'8" rookie receiver out of Louisiana Tech. Garoppolo fired six passes in Taylor's direction, and all six were caught. Five of those receptions came on third down, including a 33-yard catch and run that kept the 49ers' winning drive going and set up the game-winning field goal from Robbie Gould against his former team, the Chicago Bears.

The winning continued the next week on the road against the Houston Texans and the week after that in a home game against a Tennessee Titans team that would later make the playoffs. An even bigger test occurred the following week when another playoff-bound team, the Jacksonville Jaguars, rolled into town. Jacksonville had a 10–4 record and the top scoring defense in the league at the time. But it couldn't cool off Garoppolo and the 49ers, who scored 44 points. One of the touchdowns came on another magician-like throw from Garoppolo, who had to wing a sidearm pass to Taylor to get around an oncoming rusher. That blind, off-balance throw ended up being a five-yard touchdown. Levi's

Stadium, which had been barely half full since its inaugural season in 2014 and had developed a reputation as a vanilla place to see a game, was loud, electric, and full as the 49ers outpaced the Jaguars. It seemed like the 49ers finally had found a starting quarterback. Garoppolo Mania was in full force.

That excitement paused the following season. Garoppolo tore his ACL in the third game and was lost for the season. The 49ers had one win at that point and only would get three more the rest of the year. But the season wasn't an entire washout. The unity the team had shown during the early stages of 2017 remained in place. A number of young players also were thrown into the mix, gaining valuable experience along the way. The team's first-round draft pick, Mike McGlinchey, started all 16 games at right tackle. Linebacker Fred Warner, a third-round pick, played more than 1,000 defensive snaps.

The young player who truly emerged, however, was Kittle. He had an 82-yard catch and run in Week Four, in which he put a move on the Los Angeles' Chargers deep safety and then outran him to the end zone. He had a 71-yard play in a Week Nine win against the Oakland Raiders. In Week 14 against the Denver Broncos, Kittle had plays of 85, 52, and 31 yards by halftime and finished with a career high 210 receiving yards on the afternoon. Kittle not only became the 49ers' leading receiver that season, but he also became the league's best tight end. He was capable of pancaking defenders in the running game and scoring touchdowns from any point on the field. And as the team entered its finale against the Rams in Los Angeles, he was 100 yards from setting the single-season record for receiving yards by a tight end that previously had been held by New England's Rob Gronkowski. The 49ers had long been eliminated from the playoffs. A win against the Rams—and a record for Kittle—was what was at stake.

They ended up getting one of the two. Earlier in the day, Kansas City Chiefs tight end Travis Kelce actually had taken the record from

Gronkowski with a 62-yard effort against the Raiders. Kittle ended up surpassing Kelce's new mark late in the fourth quarter. Shanahan called a timeout before a second-down play at the Los Angeles 43-yard line. On the next snap, quarterback Nick Mullens fired a short pass to Kittle, who made the first defender miss and then—as had been the case on so many plays that season—outraced the rest of the defense to the end zone.

He passed Kelce on that play, had 149 yards that afternoon, and finished with 1,377 yards for the season, which comfortably gave him the single-season mark for a tight end. "We told him that as soon as he gets [the record], we're done," said Shanahan, who said he was intent on getting his starters off the field so late in the contest. "So it was pretty cool that he turned it into a touchdown. But that's what he's been doing all year. He's done a hell of a job."

The final thing the 49ers accomplished in 2018 was being bad. The team lost the finale to the Rams and in doing so secured the No. 2 overall pick in the draft. That meant that if a quarterback was taken with the first pick—which had been the case in seven of the last 10 drafts—the 49ers had an excellent shot at getting the best player available. That's exactly what happened. After finding a quarterback in 2017 and bolstering the offensive line the next year, the team's focus in 2019 was its defensive line. The 49ers started by hiring perhaps the most intense and animated position coach in the league, Kris Kocurek, who implemented a Wide Nine alignment that demanded his linemen be quick and aggressive off the snap. For decades stopping the run was the top criterion for defenses. The Wide Nine recognized that the NFL had become a pass-first league, and that getting to the quarterback needed to be the highest priority. The 49ers' next move was to trade for Dee Ford, who at about 245 pounds was light for a traditional defensive end but whose burst from the line of scrimmage was like a sprinter out of the starting blocks. He would line up on one edge of the 49ers' defensive line. Who would be his bookend on the other side?

For that the 49ers turned to their No. 2 overall draft pick. Ohio State defensive end Nick Bosa was the easy choice. He had been injured for most of his final college season, but the risk of picking him No. 2 overall was mitigated by how similar he was to his brother, Joey, who had been the No. 3 overall pick by the Chargers three years earlier. They played the same position, went to the same school, had the same training regimen. They even wore the same number at Ohio State. If you were watching a film clip and saw No. 97 in an Ohio State uniform swipe away the hands of an offensive tackle and then crash into the back of the quarterback, you had to be pretty astute to tell if you were looking at Joey or Nick.

Joey was named the NFL's Defensive Rookie of the Year after his first season, and midway through the 2019 year, it looked like Nick would be a shoe-in for the same award. He seemed to be everywhere on the field and on top of that he was more of a showman than his older brother. During a *Monday Night Football* game against the Cleveland Browns early in the season, he knocked down Cleveland quarterback Baker Mayfield at the end of the game and then punctuated the play by pantomiming someone planting a flag, which is what Mayfield had done when his Oklahoma team beat Bosa's Ohio State squad two years earlier. "Everybody knows what that was for," Bosa said, "just wanted to get payback. He had it coming."

Two weeks later Bosa again was on the front of the sports page and leading off highlight shows after celebrating a late-game sack against the Washington Redskins by sliding—on his belly—across an exceedingly wet and muddy field in Landover, Maryland. The rest of the defense, as well as a dozen 49ers standing on the sideline, joined him with their own joyous belly slides. Back home the next week against the Carolina Panthers, there was yet another Bosa moment. He leaped into the air to snatch an outlet pass and then nearly galloped all the way in the other direction for a touchdown. He and the 49ers defense, especially the revamped defensive line, were conspicuous as the team roared out to an 8–0 record to begin the 2019 season.

The offense had its moments, too. Garoppolo, who was coming back from his ACL tear, shook off a slow start and especially heated up after the 49ers traded for veteran receiver Emmanuel Sanders in October. The team then had a memorable month of December, in which all five games came down to the final seconds. The first ended in a loss to the Baltimore Ravens when Justin Tucker kicked a 49-yard game-winning field goal as time expired. The next week the 49ers were in New Orleans, and this time it was their chance to boot in a game winner with the clock winding down. The key play came on fourth and 2 at the San Francisco 33-yard line with the 49ers trailing the New Orleans Saints 46–45 with 39 seconds to play.

Shanahan called an option route for Kittle, who could either break inside or outside depending on how he was being covered on the play. Both he and Garoppolo read it correctly, and he caught the short pass for a first down and a lot more than that. Kittle refused to be taken down by one defender and furiously charged down the sideline with three Saints tugging, pulling, and otherwise struggling to drag him down. When a facemask penalty against New Orleans was tacked on to the play, Kittle had picked up 53 yards, setting up Gould for an easy game-winning kick. "Nothing embodies who he is more than that New Orleans play," Lynch said of Kittle. "I mean, I talk to old timers, and they always say he's like Mike Ditka. They say that's how Mike Ditka was as a player, but maybe George is a little faster. That play was fourth and 2, and in that moment, he basically willed us to win. But he does that in every part of his game— whether it's run blocking or whether it's catching a ball like that. He's awesome."

The final big play of the regular season belonged to a defensive rookie. This time it wasn't Bosa. Instead, inside linebacker Dre Greenlaw, who like Kittle had been a fifth-round pick, lowered his shoulder and stopped a Seattle Seahawks tight end from scoring a game-winning touchdown on Seattle's final snap of the game. The Seahawks had all the momentum in the game and all the momentum on the play. Quarterback Russell Wilson hit Jacob Hollister in stride, and it looked as if he would power into the end zone. Greenlaw, however, had planted himself on the goal line and stopped Hollister cold, dropping him perhaps an inch from the end zone line. The massive hit ended the 49ers' dubious losing streak in Seattle, one that had begun when Jim Harbaugh was the coach seven years earlier. More importantly, it delivered a win that secured the No. 1 seed in the NFC, which the 49ers rode to the Super Bowl.

That's when the good vibrations of the 2019 season came to a sudden halt. The 49ers lost a 10-point lead in the fourth quarter and fell to the Chiefs 31–20. During the year there were all sorts of comparisons as far as which previous 49ers squad the 2019 version was most like. Was it the 1981 team, who two years earlier had hired an offensive-minded genius in Bill Walsh and acquired a handsome, hard-to-rattle Italian American quarterback in Joe Montana? Or was the 2019 squad more like the 2012 team led by Harbaugh that had a stout defense and an equally strong offense, though it couldn't quite put it all together and became the franchise's first team to lose a Super Bowl?

In the end 2019 turned out most like the 2011 season because it was so much fun for everyone involved. The climb to the top always is the most enjoyable part of the journey, and it's one that players have said they'll remember and cherish for the rest of their lives. And they say it's just the start of a new era. "Every single day I came to work, I enjoyed it," Kittle said. "The work ethic and the mind-set of the guys around here, the selflessness, I think that will speak volumes. If guys treat [this off-season] the right way, we'll have every opportunity in the world to make it back."

ACKNOWLEDGMENTS

In the 1989 movie *Parenthood*, the main character, Gil, who's played by Steve Martin, is having an animated debate with his wife about whether to have another child, which the easily frazzled Gil thinks will make their already topsy-turvy life more chaotic. Gil's grandmother overhears them, meanders into the room, and launches into a story about a roller coaster. "When I was 19, Grandpa took me on a roller coaster," she said sweetly. "Up, down, up, down. Oh, what a ride!"

"What a great story," said Gil while practically rolling his eyes.

The grandmother didn't pay attention. "I always wanted to go again," she continued. "It was just so interesting to me that a ride could make me so frightened, so scared, so sick, so excited, and so thrilled all together! Some didn't like it. They went on the merry-go-round. That just goes around. Nothing. I like the roller coaster. You get more out of it."

It's a great way to describe the San Francisco 49ers of the 21st century. No, they haven't won a Super Bowl. And, yes, they've left you dizzy, depleted, and sick to your stomach at times. But they've been compelling.

That begins with the personalities.

To cover Jim Harbaugh's teams—on which this book was largely based—was to be thrown to one side of the car and then to the other. He could be grumpy, curt, funny, warm, expansive, obtuse, and childish— sometimes in the same press conference.

One day in the summer of 2012, Harbaugh burst into an end-of-practice press conference. He wasn't scheduled to speak that day, but there he was walking stridently to the podium. None of the reporters knew what was happening, but we all got our pens ready. "I just want to update you on the status of A.J. Jenkins," Harbaugh said with emotion in his voice while discussing the team's rookie wide receiver, who had been chosen in the first round a few months earlier. "A.J. Jenkins was an outstanding football player when he got here."

Was? Why was Harbaugh using the past tense? Had Jenkins quit? Had he gotten hurt? Had he gotten into a bad car accident? No,

Harbaugh merely was warming up. He had taken the microphone to chastise reporters about their harsh coverage of Jenkins, who hadn't been very good thus far in practices. And he obviously had been rehearsing his lines. "For those—the scribes, pundits, so-called experts—who have gone so far as to say that he's going to be a bust, they should just stop," Harbaugh lectured. "I recommend that because they're making themselves look more clueless than they already did. I'll go on record: A.J. is going to be an outstanding football player."

Harbaugh was wrong, of course. Jenkins was traded a year later without ever having made a catch for the 49ers. He fizzled out of the NFL shortly after that. But that's not the point. The point is that Harbaugh could sound like a jerk sometimes, but he was always interesting. The roller-coaster ride he took everyone on led to interesting stories, drama-rich seasons, and to, hopefully, a good book.

So thank you to all the unique personalities I've covered over the years, a group that begins with Harbaugh and also includes Mike Nolan, Norv Turner, Mike Singletary, Mike Martz, and Vic Fangio.

Special thanks to Joe Staley, who serves as the bookends in this story because he was the lone 49er who played in both of the team's Super Bowls this century. No one has taken the turns, the dips, and the ascents for as long as Staley, who was both the funniest guy in the locker room and one of the most observant.

Staley wrote the foreword to this book and also sat down with me for three, long interviews—his only recompense was a lunch in Boardman, Ohio—to go over his memories of the Harbaugh-era 49ers. Thanks also to public relations man Mike Chasanoff, who sat in on those sessions and who was excellent at recalling scores and situations that kept the conversations accurate and on track.

This book is largely built on 25 interviews I conducted. Alex Smith and his wife, Liz, were particularly generous with their time, especially considering that Alex was rehabilitating from a frightening leg injury when we spoke. Thanks also to Justin Smith, Jonathan Goodwin, and Carlos Rogers for their recollections. Goodwin did his over the phone with a fussy baby in his arms.

Greg Roman, the team's former offensive coordinator, was especially valuable because of his impressive recall. Roman not only could remember the play he dialed up at a critical moment of a particular game, but also the down and distance, where all 22 players were aligned, and how much time was remaining. After a few conversations, you begin to realize why certain people are so good at their jobs.

Thanks to Bill Ames from Triumph Books for persistently pursuing me about writing this book and to my book editor, Jeff Fedotin, for extending my deadline. (We didn't know that the 2019 49ers were going all the way to the Super Bowl.) Also, thanks to my editor at The Athletic, Tim Kawakami, who probably didn't love the fact that his 49ers writer was churning out a 70,000-word book at the same time the Bay Area's favorite team was marching toward a playoff berth but who never uttered an irritated word.

Finally, and most importantly, thanks to my parents. Growing up in Centreville, Virginia, autumn Sundays were divided into three parts: a nature walk in the morning, a Washington Redskins game in the afternoon, and a big, family dinner at the end of the day. Those have remained the three pillars of my life even if the shades of red and gold have changed over the years. We began watching those games as a family in the late 1970s, which preceded the era of elaborate end-zone celebrations and sack dances. Back then, if a camera caught a player on the bench, he'd merely wave and say, "Hi, Mom!"

At which point, my own mother would turn to me and say, "I expect you to do the same when you become an NFL player."

I'm still working on it, Mom, but it's possible that this is the best you're going to get.

SOURCES

I'm Just a Kicker by Owen Pochman
NFL.com
NFLGsis.com
Profootballreference.com
Sports Illustrated
The Athletic
The Sacramento Bee
The Washington Post

ABOUT THE
AUTHOR

Matt Barrows has covered the San Francisco 49ers since 2003, a span that has included seven head coaches, two trips to the Super Bowl, and a pair of two-win seasons. He was a reporter with *The Sacramento Bee* for 19 years, four of them as a metro reporter. Before that he spent two years in South Carolina covering county-level politics for *The (Hilton Head) Island Packet*. He has degrees from the University of Virginia and Northwestern's Medill School of Journalism.